For Gill, Andrew and David, with all my love.

Acknowledgments

To my brothers Peter and Mike, and to Barnaby Gordon: for their help, encouragement and enthusiasm.

To all the fans of Porcupine Tree: for keeping the flame alive.

Thanks to Gill and Andrew for being vigilant and patient proofreaders and the kindest of critics. And to David, for listening patiently as always.

And special thanks to Steven Wilson and the other members of Porcupine Tree: without whom...

Would you like to write for Sonicbond Publishing?

We are mainly a music publisher, but we also occasionally publish in other genres including film and television. At Sonicbond Publishing we are always on the look-out for authors, particularly for our two main series, On Track and Decades.

Mixing fact with in depth analysis, the On Track series examines the entire recorded work of a particular musical artist or group. All genres are considered from easy listening and jazz to 60s soul to 90s pop, via rock and metal.

The Decades series singles out a particular decade in an artist or group's history and focuses on that decade in more detail than may be allowed in the On Track series.

While professional writing experience would, of course, be an advantage, the most important qualification is to have real enthusiasm and knowledge of your subject. First-time authors are welcomed, but the ability to write well in English is essential.

Sonicbond Publishing has distribution throughout Europe and North America, and all our books are also published in E-book form. Authors will be paid a royalty based on sales of their book. Further details about our books are available from www.sonicbondpublishing.com. To contact us, complete the contact form there or email info@sonicbondpublishing.co.uk

on track ...

Porcupine Tree

Contents

on track ...
Porcupine Tree

every album, every song

Nick Holmes

sonicbondpublishing.com

Sonicbond Publishing Limited
www.sonicbondpublishing.co.uk
Email: info@sonicbondpublishing.co.uk

First Published in the United Kingdom 2021
First Published in the United States 2021

British Library Cataloguing in Publication Data:
A Catalogue record for this book is available from the British Library

Copyright Nick Holmes 2021

ISBN 978-1-78952-144-3

Typeset in ITC Garamond & ITC Avant Garde
Printed and bound in England

Graphic design and typesetting: Full Moon Media

Introduction

Porcupine Tree began almost as a joke in 1987, when Steven Wilson and his friend, Malcolm Stocks, decided to start a fictitious band. Inspiration came from one of Steven's favourite groups, XTC, who in 1984 formed an imaginary psychedelic band called The Dukes of Stratosphear. The band was made up of members of XTC given fictitious names, like Sir John Johns and Lord Cornelius Plum. They played music inspired by the late 1960s and were initially marketed as a mysterious new act.

Following XTC's example, Steven invented fictitious members for his own band, Porcupine Tree: Sir Tarquin Underspoon, Timothy Tadpole-Jones, Sebastian Tweetle-Blampton III, and a drummer called The Expanding Flan. Although the band consisted only of Steven Wilson recording in his bedroom at his parents' house, he took it seriously enough that he decided to record several hour's worth of material.

Steven released a series of recordings on cassette, under the Porcupine Tree name: *Tarquin's Seaweed Farm (Words from a Hessian Sack)* (1989), *The Nostalgia Factory (and other tips for amateur golfers)* (1990) and *The Love, Death & Mussolini* EP (1990). To preserve the joke, Steven also invented an extensive discography and a long history for the Porcupine Tree. Simultaneously, Steven formed an art rock band with No-Man singer Tim Bowness and violinist Ben Coleman. The band signed to an indie record label now known as One Little Independent Records, whose roster included Björk. But despite early promise and high praise from the press, the group achieved only modest success. Wilson and Bowness continued as a duo, releasing several studio albums.

In early 1989, Steven started sending out copies of *Tarquin's Seaweed Farm* to various people he thought might be interested. The cassette caught the attention of Richard Allen and Ivor Trueman, who produced an underground magazine called *Freakbeat*. They were in the process of starting a new record label called Delerium. They agreed to put one of Steven's songs on their first release: a compilation of music by psychedelic groups. Delerium also reissued the first two Porcupine Tree cassettes.

Steven was invited to sign to the Delerium label, and he compiled some of the material he'd already released, into a double album called *On the Sunday of Life*. Although it was under the band name, Porcupine Tree, it was still a solo project. The record was released in early 1992 in a limited edition of 1,000 copies, which sold out very quickly. The album was reissued, and by the end of the decade, had sold 20,000 copies.

In late 1992, Steven released the single 'Voyage 34', which was originally to be part of another double album. The eventual release – *Up the Downstair* (1993) – did not include 'Voyage 34' and was a single album rather than a double. Although Porcupine Tree was still a solo project, the record did include guest contributions from future band members Richard Barbieri and Colin Edwin. In December 1994, further songs from the *Up the Downstair* sessions were released, as the *Staircase Infinities* EP – a limited edition of 2,000 – later released on CD.

In 1993, Steven decided he wanted to play the Porcupine Tree music live, and he got together a band consisting of himself on guitar and vocals, Barbieri on keyboards, Edwin on bass, and Chris Maitland on drums. They made their debut on 4 December 1993 at the Nag's Head pub in High Wycombe, England, in front of a crowd of about 200 people.

The next album – *The Sky Moves Sideways* (1995) – marked a crucial transition in the band's history. Steven had already recorded part of the album when he invited the others to join the band. Rather than being a solo project with the occasional guest, Porcupine Tree now had permanent members. The album was also the band's first release in America.

The first Porcupine Tree album to feature all four band members on the entire record was *Signify* in 1996. The band embarked on a highly successful European tour, and in March 1997, played in front of 5,000 fans over three nights in Rome.

With the band's increasing success, Delerium Records felt they didn't have the resources to support the band's increasing profile. Porcupine Tree parted amicably from the label, and Richard Allen continued to help managing them.

1998 was spent recording the next album. It took a little while to find a new label, but eventually, a deal was signed with the independent, Snapper. The first release was *Stupid Dream* in 1999. The band toured extensively throughout Europe to support the album, and also toured America for the first time.

In early 2000, *Lightbulb Sun* was released, and further extensive touring of Europe and America continued into the next year. Porcupine Tree played at European festivals and also supported American progressive metal band Dream Theater, on a major tour.

The band's only line-up change occurred in February 2002, when drummer Chris Maitland left to be replaced by Gavin Harrison. Around that time, the band signed a new deal with Lava Records: part of the major label, Atlantic Records. For the first time, Porcupine Tree had substantial financial backing and travelled to New York to record the next album: *In Absentia*. It was released in America in September 2002 and in Europe in January 2003. On various tours promoting the album, guitarist/vocalist John Wesley, augmented the band. *In Absentia* was the band's most successful release at that stage, selling over 100,000 copies in the first year.

The next album – *Deadwing* – released in 2005 proved to be the band's last record on Lava, as Atlantic decided to close the label down. Porcupine Tree then signed with Roadrunner Records, and the band began the final and most commercially successful period of their career. In early 2007, *Fear of a Blank Planet* was released. It was Grammy-nominated (Best Surround Sound Album), and readers of *Classic Rock* magazine voted it Album Of The Year. It reached number 31 in the UK charts and 59 in the US. That September, the band released the mini-album, *Nil Recurring*, consisting of additional tracks recorded during the *Fear of a Blank Planet* sessions.

The final Porcupine Tree album – *The Incident* – was released in September 2009. It was also nominated for the Best Surround Sound Grammy. It reached number 23 in the UK and 25 in America.

But Porcupine Tree did not officially split up. They last played live at London's Royal Albert Hall on 14 October 2010, and haven't recorded any new material since *The Incident*. Rumours circulating about possible tours, have come to nothing: at least at the time of this writing (July 2021). Steven Wilson has pursued a successful solo career since 2008, but countless fans would love to see the band perform live again.

Cast of Characters

Steven Wilson (born 1967)

Singer, guitarist, keyboard player, founder member and main songwriter for Porcupine Tree. As a child, Steven was forced to learn the guitar and piano, but gave up, as he was not enjoying it. At the age of eleven, he found an acoustic guitar in his parents' attic and began experimenting with multitrack recording. His father, an electronics engineer, built Steven a four-track recorder, and also a primitive sequencer that divided bars up into units of three and nine, rather than the usual four and eight; perhaps instilling in Steven a love of prog rock's unusual time signatures.

In bands at school, Steven started his mid-teens with Karma and Altamont, the latter later morphing into the Bass Communion ambient project. He's also released psychedelic material under the name I.E.M. (Incredible Expanding Mindfuck). He has collaborated with Tim Bowness (No-Man), Aviv Geffen (Blackfield) and Mikael Åkerfeldt (Storm Corrosion). Steven has worked extensively as a producer for both Porcupine Tree and Opeth, and has remixed several classic albums, sometimes in surround sound.

Steven's solo career began in 2008 while he was still a Porcupine Tree member, and he's since written and produced six studio albums. His most recent – *To the Bone* (2017) and The *Future Bites* (2021) – both reached the UK top five.

Richard Barbieri (born 1957)

Keyboard player for Porcupine Tree, Barbieri was a founder member of the art-rock band Japan, and also performed with their later incarnation, Rain Tree Crow. He first worked with Steven Wilson on the tour to promote No-Man's debut mini-album. He does not regard himself as a technically gifted player but is highly skilled at programming synths to produce very evocative sounds and textures. He has released a number of albums under his own name.

Chris Maitland (born 1964)

Porcupine Tree's drummer until February 2002. Before Chris joined the band, he worked with Steven Wilson as the drummer for No-Man on their autumn 1993 tour. After he left Porcupine Tree, he played drums on the first Blackfield album in 2003. A skilful musician, he brought huge power and excitement to the band.

Gavin Harrison (born 1963)

Gavin became Porcupine Tree's drummer in February 2002. He is a highly-skilled, technical and physically powerful drummer, who has written books on drum technique. He is very highly regarded, and has been voted Drummer of the Year several times by readers of *Prog* magazine. He's toured extensively with King Crimson and is a member of The Pineapple Thief. He's released albums under his own name and with bass player Antoine Fafard.

Colin Edwin (born 1970)

Bass player, Colin Edwin, was born in Melbourne, Australia, but has lived just north of London for most of his life. An accomplished player, he comes from a musical family. His father played jazz guitar, his sisters studied music formally, and his brother studied classical guitar at university. He has an extensive discography outside of Porcupine Tree, having released several solo albums. Colin has also worked with Tim Bowness, and more recently with O.R.K and Eternal Return, among many others.

John Wesley (born 1962)

Guitar player and singer John Wesley became a 'fifth member' of Porcupine Tree later in their career. Steven Wilson first met John when producing an album for Marillion singer Fish, and John was hired as guitar player on the subsequent tour. John joined Porcupine Tree as an additional vocalist and guitarist for a short American tour in July 2002, prior to the release of *In Absentia*. His guitar and backing vocals enabled the live band to reproduce the complex, layered parts from the studio albums.

Lasse Hoile (born 1973)

The other person with a claim to being Porcupine Tree's 'fifth member' is Danish artist, photographer and filmmaker, Lasse Hoile. He started working with the band as a photographer for the *In Absentia* album cover, quickly developing the ability to translate Steven Wilson's thoughts into striking and often disturbing visual imagery. He provided photographs for the albums and made films used as projections in the band's shows, giving the band a strong visual identity.

On the Sunday of Life (1992)

Personnel:
Steven Wilson: vocals and all instruments, except:
John Marshall: drums on 'Third Eye Surfer'
Solomon St. Jermain (Malcolm Stocks): additional guitar and voice on 'Queen Quotes Crowley'
Master Timothy Masters: oboe
Recorded at: No Man's Land, Hemel Hempstead, Hertfordshire, England, 1988-1991
Producer: Steven Wilson
Release date: July 1992
Chart placings: Did not chart
Running Time: 75:47
Record label: Delerium
Current edition: Kscope

On the Sunday of Life is the first Porcupine Tree studio album. As described in the Introduction, the band was originally fictitious: a cover for Steven Wilson's solo studio projects. He didn't plan to release any of the early cassette albums on vinyl or CD: it appears the cassettes were released largely for his own amusement. But then his music came to the attention of Richard Allen: editor of *Freakbeat* magazine. With Ivor Trueman, Richard set up Delerium records, to release psychedelic music. Ivor had previously founded the Pink Floyd fanzine, *The Amazing Pudding*. Richard also became Porcupine Tree's manager for many years, finally parting company with them in 2004.

Porcupine Tree's first release on Delerium Records, was the track 'Linton Samuel Dawson' (from *The Nostalgia Factory)*, on a 1991 compilation called *A Psychedelic Psauna (In Four Parts)*. Most of the bands on the double LP are long forgotten, but Ozric Tentacles can be found on side four; and, as Richard Allen told Stephen Humphries in the notes for the thirteen-CD box set, *Porcupine Tree: The Delerium Years 1991-1997* released in 2020, Delerium had turned Porcupine Tree into a real band: 'I think, in the minds of people who bought it, Porcupine Tree were a bunch of way-out hippies, living in a farm somewhere and making this amazing music ... we managed to make (Steven's) joke into a reality.'

Delerium Records began when Allen and Trueman needed to produce seven-inch flexi discs to go with *Freakbeat* magazine. But the label soon became a separate entity, re-issuing *Tarquin's Seaweed Farm* and *The Nostalgia Factory* as cassette tapes, which were then deleted from the catalogue after selling around 300 copies each. Delerium's original plan was to re-issue the two albums as separate double LPs, but Steven decided it would be better to issue the strongest tracks as one album. This compilation became Porcupine Tree's first official studio release, *On the Sunday of Life*, initially on double vinyl only. The original pressing was only 1,000 copies, which took many years to sell, but according to *Prog* magazine in 2016, the album went on to sell around 30,000 copies. The remaining tracks from *Tarquin's Seaweed Farm* and *The Nostalgia Factory* were released on the *Yellow Hedgerow Dreamscape* compilation CD in 1994, in a limited edition of 2500 on the Magic Gnome label (later re-released on the Headphone Dust label).

Steven recorded the album on what he described in the notes for the 2015 CD remaster as one of 'my earliest recording setups'. He used a four-track cassette machine designed and built by his father, and later an eight-track reel-to-reel. The final stage was mixing the songs down to a reel-to-reel:

> ...a very old Revox two-track machine that had been given to me by a friend of my dad. In those days, I would quite often fill up a tape with experiments and songs, mix them down, and then rewind the tape and start again, erasing what was there before, essentially making the stereo mix done at the time – for better or worse – definitive.

The album title is taken from the 1965 French film *Le Dimanche de la Vie* – directed by Jean Herman – and was chosen from a long list of nonsense titles compiled by Richard Allen of Delerium.

Although they are all Steven Wilson songs, it's hard to pin down his songwriting voice. In November 2016 he told Dave Ling of Prog magazine that the album 'could have spawned nine or ten bands in as many different styles'. Perhaps what unites the songs at this stage is a high musical intelligence, an enquiring mind, a strong sense of melody and a sense of fun. Steven told Pete Clemons of *Coventry Music Articles Music* blogspot in 1994:

> I love the idea of making a sprawling mess of an album, and this is my favourite aspect of *On the Sunday of Life*. It covers a very wide range of moods and ideas. It is not always successful musically, or a constant listen, but it will always be one of my favourites. In making that album, I discovered the direction I wanted to take, at least for a few years.

Rather than learn his craft in the way that most bands do – playing cover versions – Steven instead learned to write by copying his predecessors' styles. As he told Steven Rosen of *Ultimate-Guitar.com* in 2011: 'The influences were more obviously referenced almost in a kind of pastiche way, which was a deliberate thing.' The source material on which he drew, was the music he'd listened to as a teenager in the 1980s:

> I went back and discovered a lot of music from ... the late '60s and early '70s ... the golden era for album-orientated music; the kind of explosion and creativity that came out of the late '60s when rock music was really raised to the level of an art form for the first time; or pop music as it was called then ... popular music became, for the first time, something that people actually would consider an intellectual pursuit. Almost anything from that era I kind of have a soft spot for.

Most of the album's lyrics were written by Alan Duffy: a school friend of Steven's with whom he'd lost touch a few years before the album was released. Steven later described him on his website as an 'English psychedelic scenester'. When Steven was fifteen, he and a childhood friend – Simon Vockings – formed a band called Altamont. They recorded only one album, on cassette: *Prayer for the Soul*, featuring lyrics by Duffy. Steven told Pete Clemons, that Alan Duffy's lyrics were written between 1983 and 1985 for a project that 'never came to much' (when he was about sixteen). A few years later – still lacking confidence in his own lyrics – he recycled Alan's old lyrics, and wrote new music for Porcupine Tree, except in the case of tracks such as 'Jupiter Island' and 'Nine Cats', where he also recycled the music. In 1985, Alan Duffy founded Imaginary Records, who released albums by The Chameleons, The Mock Turtles and Bill Nelson, among others. Steven contacted Alan briefly to sort out the publishing rights for Alan's lyrics, but there seems to have never been any suggestion that he would release Steven's music on his label.

The original sleeve design for *On the Sunday of Life* was by Mike Bennion: a director of TV commercials whom Steven collaborated with much later on the script for the *Deadwing* movie. The film itself has not yet been made – though pre-production work began in 2020 – but the script formed the basis of the 2005 Porcupine Tree album of the same name (see the chapter on *Deadwing* for more details).

The cover image is a homage to the work of Hipgnosis, who designed many of the Pink Floyd album covers. Steven told *Crohinga Well* magazine in 1992 that he liked the contrast of the joyful title of Pink Floyd's 1975 album *Wish You Were Here*: a jolly message on a postcard to friends at home, against the album cover's 'very peculiar, very alien atmosphere'. He also liked the use of two contrasting images, such as the pig flying above Battersea Power Station on the cover of Pink Floyd's *Animals* (1977). The *On the Sunday of Life* cover shows a woman diving into a rural landscape at sunset: a surreal juxtaposition made up of two photographs. It also implies something more serious lies behind the album title: which describes a period of life when the relaxation that Sunday usually brings, can be enjoyed.

All words and music by Steven Wilson, except where marked.

'Music for the Head' (2:42)

This is a fascinating choice for the opening song: an instrumental, with a low drone and a flute-like synth sound above, sounding like early Tangerine Dream. The choice probably makes more sense in the context of Wilson's description of Tangerine Dream's 1972 album *Zeit* – an early example of ambient music – as his favourite album of all time. That album's opening track – 'Birth Of Liquid Plejades' – also features a drone (created with four cellos) and high synth parts. In August 2017, Steven told Jess Thompson of *Discogs*, that *Zeit* is, 'the original and greatest ambient record, years before the notion of ambient music existed.

It's music without melody, rhythm or structure, but listening to it is like filling the room with the most beautiful and mysterious perfume.'

The obvious difference between the two tracks is their length – the Porcupine Tree track is under three minutes, whereas 'Birth of Liquid Plejades' is a true prog epic, at nearly twenty minutes. Steven adds subtle organ to the flute and electronic drone, and a synthesized plucked string instrument that sounds as if it's from India. He told Steven Rosen that the use of the drone and Indian mysticism, 'with flutes and woodwinds and psychedelic textures', was probably also unconsciously influenced by bands like Gong and Quintessence.

It's an atmospheric opener, very different from other parts of the album, creating a deep sense of mystery, intensified by the spoken words that lie so low in the mix that they're impossible to interpret properly. It's a glimpse into the direction Porcupine Tree could've taken: perhaps an ambient band, as apparently Steven's first band, Altamont, were. Steven's yearning for the ambient was eventually satisfied through the formation of one his many side-projects: Bass Communion; and his love for Tangerine Dream was celebrated in his involvement in the sixteen-CD box set of Tangerine Dream recordings – *In Search of Hades: The Virgin Recordings 1973 – 1979* (2019) – which included new stereo and surround-sound mixes of their classic 1975 albums, *Phaedra* and *Ricochet*.

'Jupiter Island' (Alan Duffy, Steven Wilson) (6:12)

Steven wrote this song when he was sixteen: one of the few surviving from that period. Although it sounds like a place in outer space, Jupiter Island is, a real island off the coast of Florida, with several rich and famous inhabitants, including golfers and tennis players. But Alan Duffy's lyrics create a magical place, a paradise on earth, or perhaps a psychedelic paradise only reached with the aid of hallucinogenic drugs (such as LSD, which makes an appearance later in the album). The word imagery is lurid and day-glo, perhaps suggesting the latter type of paradise, with lines like 'Magenta forests on a crimson sea/The electric clouds are as vivid as can be'.

Considering its six-minute length, the song is far more straightforward than many of the later Porcupine Tree tracks in which a prog epic could be compressed into a few minutes. It is a slightly extended pop song with a bouncy, infectious feel, showing that the sixteen-year-old Wilson could enjoy himself. Instrumentally, there are very few embellishments, so it feels like a pop single, despite its length. Steven told *Crohinga Well* magazine that it was 'pure psychedelic pop ... a psychedelic poem set to music'. He also admitted that the song was heavily influenced by 'Bike Ride To The Moon' by The Dukes of Stratosphear (another fictitious band). The songs share a 'kind of Syd Barrett nursery rhyme quality', contrasting with the 'incredibly politically aware ... very dark imagery' of many of Pink Floyd's lyrics.

Steven's vocals are pitch-shifted to make them sound a little higher, prompting one online forum commenter to say that at first, they thought there was a guest vocalist because the singer on this track sounds like a girl. Prince used a similar technique on his unreleased album, *Camille*, on which he created the female alter-ego Camille by speeding up the vocals. If Prince's sped-up vocals are androgynous and sexy, Steven's are simply fun.

'Third Eye Surfer' (Steven Wilson, John Marshall) (2:48)

This instrumental track was co-written with John Marshall: drummer of the jazz rock band, Nucleus, and the rock band, Soft Machine. In fact, Steven Wilson used a sample of a Marshall drum solo from Soft Machine's album, *Six* (1973). He later told Stephen Humphries that he didn't anticipate that using a sample would be a problem: 'Later on, when I became better known, I had to clear all that with John ... I was just sampling from records, to give my records a broader musical palette and a wider vocabulary of sound. It was only later that I had to go back and replace all that stuff'.

The song title refers to the third eye: the gateway to higher states of consciousness in some religions, including Hinduism. It relates to the Indian mysticism of 'Music for the Head', and more generally to the album's psychedelic themes.

The track mainly features John Marshall's jazz drumming, with keyboards from Steven, and oboe parts presumably played by Master Timothy Masters. It is an improvised piece, where texture and virtuosity are more important than melody.

'On the Sunday of Life...' (2:11)

'Third Eye Surfer' segues into this track, which is surprisingly short for an album title track. Delicate oboe flourishes lead into a brief moment of contemplation with gorgeous synth washes, followed by what is effectively a powerful drum solo, although some instrumental textures remain, floating around the drums.

'The Nostalgia Factory' (Alan Duffy, Steven Wilson) (7:25)

This is the title track of the second Porcupine Tree cassette.

In the booklet for the two-CD compilation *Stars Die: The Delerium Years 1991–1997*, the song title is explained as a satire on the 'tribute band mentality on the psychedelic scene', and also the short memories of music reviewers: Steven is quoted as saying, 'If you try to talk to the British music press about the history of music, their knowledge often doesn't go back beyond The Stone Roses or Happy Mondays'. As if to prove his point, *Melody Maker* compared 'The Nostalgia Factory' to Ride's 1992 single, 'Leave Them All Behind', whereas the true influence was The Who's 1971 single, 'Won't Get Fooled Again'. All three tracks use a very distinctive synth pattern. On the Who track, Pete Townshend used an ARP 2500 synthesizer to control chords played on a Lowry electronic organ.

Before the main synthesizer/guitar theme, the song begins with Indian-sounding instruments, giving a sense of psychedelic mysticism similar to the opener, 'Music for the Head.' This mysticism is increased by the fact that two long verses seem to be missing from the song so that all we clearly hear is the confused caterpillar story that bookends the track. The caterpillar asks the protagonist what goes on 'inside your swollen head', and is so shocked by his insight, that at the end of the song, he decides to turn into a butterfly (the butterfly returns later in 'Nine Cats'). The protagonist's trip is evidently drug-induced and so deeply buried in the mix that it's impossible to decipher the lyrics or even to be sure if they are there at all. This increases the impression that the trip is taking place in the protagonist's head, obscured from the caterpillar's (and the listener's ears). The missing words – sixteen lines in total – are available online and in the CD booklet.

'Space Transmission' (2:59)
This is not really a song; more a message from outer space. It is a genuinely creepy monologue, uttered by a creature that's been trapped on another planet 'for many aeons' by 'You know who', in complete darkness since going blind or 'since the sun exploded fourteen centuries ago'. It could've come from a Doctor Who episode – it's not difficult to imagine the song's monsters causing children to hide behind the sofa. We know nothing about 'He who keeps me here', but he regards himself as a competitor to God, so is apparently a supreme being. The protagonist seems to be a creature with 'scales', whose threats of revenge upon return to earth are as dark as the black liquid that seeps uncontrollably from its mouth.

The accompanying music is there to provide atmosphere only. If Steven had chosen to write science fiction plays for radio or TV, he could've had a completely different and equally successful career. But he abandoned the darkness of outer space, instead using songs to travel deep into the darkness of the human psyche.

'Message From a Self-Destructing Turnip' (0:27)
Like the self-destructing recorded messages in the TV show *Mission: Impossible*, the turnip counts down the five seconds to its own destruction.

'Radioactive Toy' (10:00)
Mark Radcliffe played this song on Radio One. As Steven told Stephen Humphries: 'I remember the first time my mum heard my music on BBC radio, she was really excited. Much more than I was, in fact! I think she was beginning to understand that maybe I did have something that I could develop into a career.'

According to the *Stars Die* CD booklet, this song about nuclear war was inspired by the 1984 TV movie, *Threads*, written by Barry Hines: also known for his novel, *A Kestrel for a Knave* (1968), which he helped adapt for Ken Loach's film version: *Kes* (1969). The *Threads* tag line is 'The closest you'll ever want to come to nuclear war.' The BBC commissioned it after the Director-

General, Alasdair Milne, saw the 1965 BBC docu-drama, *The War Game,* which the BBC withdrew because it was deemed 'too horrifying for the medium of broadcasting'; though it was shown in some cinemas. It's perhaps difficult now to appreciate how serious the nuclear war threat was, even as late as the mid-1980s, and Steven was very concerned about that threat.

The idea of a 'radioactive toy' providing the 'freedom to destroy' suggests the words of Robert Oppenheimer – the 'father of the atomic bomb' – who quoted from the Hindu scripture, the Bhagavad Gita: 'Now I am become Death, the destroyer of worlds,' when he witnessed the first nuclear weapon detonation on 16 July 1945. The following month, atomic bombs were dropped on Hiroshima and Nagasaki. This track is closely related to 'A Smart Kid' – from Porcupine Tree's fifth album, *Stupid Dream* – which describes the effects of nuclear war.

Lyrically, 'Radioactive Toy' is sophisticated, particularly for such an early Wilson lyric attempt. Avoiding Alan Duffy's admittedly amusing, effective and whimsical lyrics, Steven shows an early ability to elegantly encapsulate a mood or idea with great economy – as in the bleak line describing disposal of a body after a nuclear war: 'Pour me into a hole/Inform my next of kin.'

The same level of sophistication can be found in the song's structure and feel; only the first few minutes feature vocals, after which it becomes a long instrumental. The long-form song has been a feature of Steven's writing throughout his career, both with Porcupine Tree and his later solo projects. Originally – as he told *Crohinga Well* magazine – when 'Radioactive Toy' appeared on the *Tarquin's Seaweed Farm* cassette, the track was about half this length, and 'we completely re-recorded and reconstructed the music.' The song had also been part of a suite titled 'Precious Memories In Freefall', but the suite had been abandoned a long time before.

The song's bass line is reminiscent of Pink Floyd's 'Another Brick In The Wall Pt. 2' (*The Wall* (1979)): it's in the same key, although it is slower, bringing a more ominous feel. The guitar parts are in a style similar style to David Gilmour, and lyrically, the dark theme is very Floydian; which led some early Porcupine Tree fans to hope the band was the next Pink Floyd. Steven later said he was aware of the comparison, but preferred songs in which he felt he'd developed his own unique songwriting voice. This book will make the Floyd comparison at various points, so it's worth addressing it in detail now. In an article titled *Don't Hate Me: A Floyd Fan's Introduction to Porcupine Tree,* from *Spare Bricks* magazine quoted in full on the *Ministry of Information* website, Patrick Keller makes an eloquent case for the comparison, which is worth quoting:

> Wilson reacted poorly to the Floyd comparisons, and has worked ever since to shake it off however he could. Have no fear though – Porcupine Tree's music remains strongly grounded in the fundamentals that made Pink Floyd such an enduring group: strong songwriting, multifaceted lyrics, solid musicianship,

willingness to experiment, a keen sense of melody, and a focus on the darker aspects of the human condition. Many bands emulate the Floyd but miss the essence that made the group so powerful. Wilson *gets it*, more so than any other band going – I would venture. No matter how far he may veer from the style of Pink Floyd, he is never far from their spirit.

Whether or not the comparison is valid, this is the album's most satisfying track – a real highlight – giving a fascinating insight into Porcupine Tree's future direction. The band's manager – Richard Allen – said it was the song that convinced him they could be successful. In the *Stars Die* notes, he is quoted as saying the song was 'the seed of a truly great band ... the overall effect was unlike anything else around at the time, and harked back to an era when rock music was much more adventurous and elastic.' Steven's choice to include the song in the setlist for the band's first-ever live gig (December 1993), shows it was a personal favourite of his. He was still playing it twenty years later: on the 2013 tour supporting his solo album, *The Raven That Refused To Sing*.

'Nine Cats' (Alan Duffy, Steven Wilson) (3:55)

This song marks the return of the butterfly from 'The Nostalgia Factory', and also the return of Alan Duffy's psychedelic lyrics: described in the *Stars Die* booklet as a cross between Lewis Carroll and Syd Barrett. The song is delivered with a wide-eyed, whimsical nursery rhyme quality, so characteristic of many of Barrett's Pink Floyd songs. Some of the lines could've come directly from a nursery rhyme, such as: 'A minstrel bought a crooked spoon/He gave it to a blue baboon.'

Steven wrote the song at age sixteen. It begins simply enough with gentle vocals, acoustic guitar and an attractive electric guitar pattern. But it soon builds, through the addition of drums made more atmospheric through a short echo effect and Floydian guitars. It's a fascinating prototype of the mature Porcupine Tree style, in which several musical and stylistic elements blend into a new musical whole.

'Hymn' (1:14)

Another instrumental, but again with spoken words, sped up and slowed down so as to be unintelligible. The track consists largely of soundscaping but ends with bleak, desolate guitar notes crying out woefully, only once coming together to form a chord.

'Footprints' (Alan Duffy, Steven Wilson) (5:59)

Surreal imagery describes what could be a poetic experience or a drug trip. It's more likely to be the latter due to the opening description of the protagonist venturing further into his mind, hoping to find 'tangerine trees and marmalade skies and plasticine porters with looking-glass ties'. These images are taken directly from The Beatles' song, 'Lucy in the Sky with Diamonds', from their 1967 album, *Sgt. Pepper's Lonely Hearts Club Band*. Some questioned whether the song title was a reference to the drug LSD: the title's initial letters; though John Lennon made it clear his son Julian came home from school with a picture he had made with that title. John also said the surreal lyric was inspired by Lewis Carroll's novel, *Alice's Adventures in Wonderland*.

'Linton Samuel Dawson' (Alan Duffy, Steven Wilson) (3:05)

Steven told Dave Ling of *Prog* magazine in November 2016 that 'Linton Samuel Dawson' was about LSD. Alan Duffy's lyric was 'very immersed in acid culture and psychedelia; it was a 'Lucy in the Sky with Diamonds'-type thing. A lot of what we were doing were shameless pastiches.'

Steven seemed to share Alan Duffy's fascination with LSD's effect on consciousness; it was a major theme in Porcupine Tree's early work. The next album – *Up the Downstair* – was originally going to include the track, 'Voyage 34' (later released as a separate EP), which describes a bad LSD trip.

Steven made it clear to Dave Ling that the idea of taking drugs, fascinated him, but as an outsider, 'People say that a lot of great artists made their best work by using them. I don't believe that; drugs allowed them to tap into the power of dreams. But I can do that without chemicals to facilitate the process.'

The song is explicit about the effects of Linton Samuel Dawson (or LSD): he 'yields his knowledge in a phial' and 'Visits many open minds/He aids escape to tranquillity/From the boredom of mankind.'

The track begins with a brief free jazz improvisation burst lasting only about ten seconds: sounding like a completely different song. The song is straightforward, using standard chord progressions. Most striking, are the vocals, electronically treated to make Steven's voice sound much higher – as if he's just inhaled helium. This comedic effect is unusual in Steven's work. It is reminiscent of David Bowie's gnome voice on the single, 'The Laughing Gnome': originally released in 1967 without chart success, and re-released in 1973, when it reached number 6 in the UK. Vocally, perhaps a closer comparison – and possible inspiration – is what Steven described to *Discogs* in 2017, as, 'the bizarre varispeed tape experiments' of the Pink Floyd song, 'Several Species of Small Furry Animals Gathered Together in a Cave and Grooving With a Pict', from their 1969 album, *Ummagumma*. This involved slowing down the tape during recording, using a variable speed control, then playing it back at normal speed, creating the small furry animals' strange high-pitched voices. As mentioned above, Steven was later to distance himself from the obvious Pink Floyd influences. But in the *Crohinga Well* magazine interview in 1992, Steven said that *Ummagumma* had a huge effect on him: 'I always used to tell people that the main reason for Porcupine Tree coming about was an unnatural obsession with that particular Pink Floyd record.'

It ends with another brief blast of the free jazz heard at the start, suggesting the song was really only a momentary aberration – a moment of joy in the middle of something much more serious and truly avant-garde: the effect of one of the 33 delightful LSD trips that came before voyage 34.

'And the Swallows Dance Above the Sun' (Alan Duffy, Steven Wilson) (4:03)

The *Stars Die* sleeve notes say these Alan Duffy lyrics are a psychedelic poem about 'the contradictions of being trapped in boredom while surrounded by wonder'. Duffy originally titled the song 'Like Ice on the Sun' when he first sent it to Steven.

Steven's vocal delivery conjures up the lyric mood perfectly: sounding both breathless with excitement and bored due to a repetitive rhythmic and lyrical pattern, creating a trance-like effect. A drum machine provides a similar feel to James Brown's 'Funky Drummer' (1970) drum break. With the funky bass, heavy voice echo, smooth synth pads and inventive guitar parts, 'And the Swallows Dance Above the Sun' feels like a long-lost early-1990s dance classic. A pleasing set of falling chords drift languidly towards the sung title. Although it's very different from most of Steven's material written since, there are signs of a great songwriter finding his voice.

The track features a number of rather startling samples. It opens with the spoken words, 'Indecent desires': the title of a 1968 B-movie. The sample comes from the film's trailer, which 'leaves you tingling with excitement, trembling with horror and throbbing with emotion'. Another sample – 'Do you know that bad girls go to hell?' – immediately follows: taken from the trailer for the 1965 movie, *Bad Girls go Hell,* which promises 'the boldest and most intimate scenes ever shown on any screen'.

The song ends with the rather remarkable spoken line. 'I want you to put Felix's penis on me!': from the 1970 sexploitation movie, *The Amazing Transplant*, in which the central character, Arthur, has a penis transplant following the death of his friend, Felix. As a result, Arthur, horrifyingly, gains not only Felix's sexual prowess but his proclivity for sexual violence. Steven chose the line simply for its surreal properties. All three movies were under director Doris Wishman: a cult figure who was the most prolific female director of the movie sound era.

Steven Wilson told Stephen Humphries that he liked using samples because, at the time, he had no confidence in his abilities as a singer: 'I was always looking for other narrative elements that I could hang instrumental music on. A lot of that was using found voices and snatches of dialogue.'

'Queen Quotes Crowley' (3:55)

Steven recorded this track with his friend, Malcolm Stocks: also credited as Solomon St. Jermain. His backwards-playing spoken words can be heard at the beginning: if you play them backwards, he clearly says, 'The Queen quotes Crowley'. Other words are more difficult to decipher, as they are buried in the mix, but possibilities, are 'Hedgehog Pâté' and 'Cream cakes ... two cream cakes'.

This would all just be a bit of fun, but it is taken very seriously by the Centro Culturale San Giorgio, as an example of *backmasking*: the use of phrases that are presented as backwards audio. The Centro's website is massively detailed and thoroughly researched, the aim of which appears to be to protect Catholicism from the occult. The words 'the Queen quotes Crowley' are quoted as an example of a 'messaggio satanico': perhaps because occultist and self-proclaimed prophet, Aleister Crowley, has been of great interest to some rock musicians; including Led Zeppelin's Jimmy Page, who was so fascinated with Crowley that he bought his one-time home, Boleskine House; and Ozzy Osbourne, who posed the question: 'Oh Mr. Crowley, did you talk with the dead?' in his 1980 song, 'Mr. Crowley'.

Whether the 'cream cake' reference also exemplifies a satanic message is unclear; though Crowley's Eucharistic host did include communion wafers that he called 'cakes of light'. The song has a mesmeric, repetitive bass line and some lively guitar work. Interestingly, the instrumental parts work almost as well played backwards as they do forwards.

'No Luck With Rabbits' (0:45)
This instrumental is a transition into the next song. It's a cacophony of organ sounds: a bit like George Martin's fairground organ on The Beatles' song, 'Being For The Benefit Of Mr. Kite!', from *Sgt. Pepper's Lonely Hearts Club Band*. The sound of crackling vinyl heightens the nostalgic feel. Steven used the effect again on the track, 'The Yellow Windows of the Evening Train', from the final Porcupine Tree album: *The Incident*.

'Begonia Seduction Scene' (2:10)
Another instrumental track, starting with beautifully recorded acoustic and electric guitars: sweet enough, no doubt, to seduce any begonia. But all is not well in this paradise garden. A malevolent synthesizer creeps in, hinting at the 'Mars, the Bringer of War' movement from Gustav Holst's orchestral suite, *The Planets* (1916).

'This Long Silence' (Alan Duffy, Steven Wilson) (5:10)
This song begins, bouncing along like one of The Cure's happier songs, with a touch of the sparkling synths of Scritti Politti's *Cupid & Psyche 85* (1985). Steven has never hidden his admiration for 1980s art rock and pop. He has remixed classic albums by not only the likes of Jethro Tull, Yes, King Crimson and Tangerine Dream, but also Ultravox and Tears for Fears. Steven also covered The Cure track, 'A Forest' on his 2010 solo album, *Cover Version*.

The lyrics are a surreal combination of cultural references, naming a mix of mythical and real figures. The humour is dark at times: for instance, Ruth Ellis – the last woman hanged in the United Kingdom – is described as blowing a kiss as she swings from the rope; and Mozart is described as being murdered in his garden by 'a systematic killer returning from Madrid'. At the end, it becomes clear that all this surreal imagery comes from the 'third eye on the surface (that) opens up my mind'. The general overall feel is more surreal than horrifying, even when John Lennon's murderer is mentioned: 'Mark Chapman stared at Fantasy/Bare wires burned in his brain.' When Steven took over lyric-writing duties on subsequent Porcupine Tree albums, the lyrics became much darker: the murderer and serial killer references on *In Absentia* (ten years later) are far from Alan Duffy's gentle whimsy.

'It Will Rain for a Million Years' (Alan Duffy, Steven Wilson) (10:47)

The album's final song is beautifully structured, with stately drums and evocative guitars. It feels like a film score, with a suitably widescreen sound and epic scope. There is also excellent bass-playing, showing that Steven wasn't completely overshadowed by Colin Edwin's talents (or later, Nick Beggs, on Wilson's solo albums).

The track is largely instrumental; the lyrics, spoken, rather than sung: many tracks on this album have either spoken-word or heavily-manipulated vocals, suggesting that Steven wasn't yet entirely confident in his vocal technique.

Lyrically, the protagonist is leaving Earth, presumably because there's been a war or natural disaster that's left the planet in such a dystopian state, that the rain will never stop. He's leaving in a spaceship; and in the opening lines, there are echoes of the David Bowie persona, Major Tom (from 'Space Oddity' and others): 'I locked myself inside the capsule/And watched the planet slowly turning blue.' Bowie's song describes the lonely Major Tom as being in a 'capsule', and the protagonists of *both* songs, observe that planet Earth looks 'blue'. The two songs share a sense of melancholy due to the inability to return to Earth, though for different reasons. The protagonist in the Porcupine Tree song, will visit 'worlds of crystal beauty' but will never find answers, suggesting that his quest is existential rather than simply an escape from a ruined planet.

Up the Downstair (1993)

Personnel:

Steven Wilson: vocals, various instruments

Richard Barbieri: electronics on 'Up the Downstair'

Colin Edwin: bass on 'Always Never'

Suzanne Barbicri: voice on 'Up the Downstair'

Gavin Harrison: drums on remixed and remastered version (2005)

Recorded at No Man's Land, Hemel Hempstead, Hertfordshire, England – February 1992 to January 1993

Producer: Steven Wilson

Release date: May 1993; re-released May 2005 with second CD (originally released in 1995 as *Staircase Infinities*)

Remixing, remastering and partial re-recording for 2005 re-release: Steven Wilson

Chart placings: Did not chart

Running time: 47:53

Record label: Delerium Records

Current edition: Kscope

Up the Downstair is Porcupine Tree's second studio album and is dedicated to 'Terumi and the spirit of Orson Welles.' The cover quotes French painter Francis Picabia: 'There is only one movement and that is perpetual motion.' (1912)

Melody Maker praised the record as 'A psychedelic masterpiece ... one of the albums of the year'. But, as Steven Wilson told Stephen Humphries in the notes for the thirteen-CD box set, *Porcupine Tree: The Delerium Years 1991-1997*, released in 2020, the record's failure to chart gave him creative freedom for the rest of his career, which might've been compromised had there been early success. It meant that he didn't have to write 'contrived mainstream music' and could do what he wanted: 'I'm just going to do what comes naturally, and if that's a 30-minute ambient piece or a three-minute pop tune, so be it.'

According to Steven's website, the album title comes from the 1967 Robert Mulligan movie, *Up the Down Staircase.* The film stars Sandy Dennis as a newly-qualified teacher starting her career at a troubled New York City high school: its separate up-and-down staircases providing the title. There is also another source for the title: a spoken-word quote from the track 'Voyage 34' (a song describing the 34th LSD trip after 33 uneventful ones; the protagonist meeting himself coming back) that was originally going to appear on the album. The effect on the character is devastating – a trip from which he never recovers: 'But on voyage 34, he finally met himself coming down an up staircase, and the encounter was crushing.'

Up the Downstair is almost entirely a Steven Wilson solo project. On two tracks, future band members joined him for the first time. Bass player Colin Edwin played on 'Always Never' about a year before he joined the band. On the band's website, he later said he was pleased to be asked to record with Steven, as he'd been 'playing in a blues band for about two years, and they never went into the studio'. He said he played to an instrumental backing track and 'never got to hear the lyrics or vocals until Steven gave me a copy of the CD, long after'.

Keyboard player Richard Barbieri – who'd already been working with Steven on his and singer Tim Bowness' No-Man project – was asked to provide 'spacey electronics' on the title track. He was happy that he used 'my old analogue synths and went to town so to speak, overlaying various electronics and effects'.

The most striking aspect of the original version of *Up the Downstair* is the lack of real drums. On the band's website, Wilson later said, 'I have some trouble listening to this album now because of the drum machines. The way I used them on the first album and the (Voyage) '34' single was more in a stylised way, but here I was trying to make them sound like a real drummer – with limited success.'

In 2005, Steven rectified the drum problem, replacing them with the newly-recorded live drums of Gavin Harrison, who'd joined the band (replacing Chris Maitland) for 2002's *In Absentia*. Steven said that he needed to replace some drum-loop samples but that the real point was to replace the drum machine: 'Gavin made it sound human and organic; less like an album of glorified demos'.

Up the Downstair was originally going to be a double album including the 'Voyage 34' single. Additional recorded material was released in 1995 as the EP, *Staircase Infinities*. In 2005, the album was partially re-recorded, fully remixed, remastered, and reissued along with the *Staircase Infinities* EP as a double album.

'What You Are Listening To...' (0:57)

Wilson told Stephen Humphries that short instrumental tracks like these, '... serve as a breathing space between the substantial works. I liked the idea of giving them titles. In naming them and making them part of the tracklisting, you're telling the audience, 'these tracks may be short and incidental, but they're just as important to the overall musical journey'.

On the band's website, he expressed satisfaction with the album's musical journey: 'This album had a lovely shape to it, and was a good balance between vocal and instrumental sections. To some extent, I don't feel we got this balance right again until *Lightbulb Sun* (the band's sixth album, released in 2000)'.

The track ends with a spoken-word sample: 'What you are listening to are musicians performing psychedelic music under the influence of a mind-altering chemical called....' The sample coyly leaves out the missing word, wittily going straight into the next track, leaving the listener guessing. The sample came from a 1966 documentary album called *LSD* (see 'Voyage 34' below). The missing word is, unsurprisingly, LSD.

'Synesthesia' (5:11)

Synesthesia – or 'union of the senses' – occurs when one sensory brain pathway is involuntarily linked to another. Letters or numbers may always be linked to a specific colour. In the case of music, vivid colours are seen when certain notes or keys are heard. Research has shown that taking LSD could have a similar effect to synesthesia in that it adds to the listening experience. Frederick Barrett, of Johns Hopkins University School of Medicine, told Eric W. Dolan of *PsyPost* in February 2020, that 'Music ... engages a broad range of brain regions involved in memory, emotion, attention, and self-directed thought. LSD increases the degree to which these brain areas process music, and it seems to use a brain mechanism that is shared across all psychedelic drugs.' The track begins with a repeated trance-like motif, which seems to suggest the LSD influence.

Instead of continuing the synesthesia theme, the track delivers what the liner notes for *Stars Die* describe as, a 'hallucinatory vision of war and death'. Although the constant repeating motif has a hypnotic effect, the lyrics paint a poignant and realistic (rather than hallucinatory) picture of an unnamed soldier facing imminent death. The soldier writes a letter to a loved one, as he looks back over his life, to clear his mind and face his responsibilities: 'Time to clear the cobwebs/Time to bear the crime'. Despite what he's been told, he knows he's about to die, as his 'back is full of lead'.

There is a play on the different meanings of the word 'lying': 'I'm lying on a stretcher/They're lying to my face.' The authorities lying to the protagonist, treat him as a number, not as a person; heartlessly sending his relatives a telegram, rather than a personalised letter that would express true sorrow: 'It's only a number/It's only a death/Another soldier died in action/The telegram regrets.'

The track ends with a soaring and uplifting guitar solo and the words, 'feeling good'. Perhaps the soldier is on strong painkillers, hallucinating as he passes into death.

'Monuments Burn Into Moments' (0:20)

A short instrumental link, this features tapes played backwards, in a technique The Beatles often used.

'Always Never' (Alan Duffy, Steven Wilson) (6:58)

This is one of a number of the album's tracks with lyrics by Alan Duffy, who also wrote most of the previous album's lyrics. The song is about different relationship stages, compressed into two lines: 'I love you sometimes/Always never'. The relationship is over now, and the narrator feels completely alienated from the lyric's addressee, and has become emotionally detached. There is a slightly puzzling reference to a third person – a male – who said, 'You're here with me now'. It's unclear who that person is, and whether the 'you' is the song's addressee, or the narrator himself

This track marks Colin Edwin's debut with the band. Steven Wilson told Stephen Humphries, 'Colin was a bass player and I wasn't. I wanted the music to have more of a band identity ... I was boring myself by doing everything on my own ... Whereas I might have just played something quick and dirty on the track, Colin added a more thoughtful approach.' The bass is less prominent than on many later tracks, but it's an auspicious start, demonstrating the invention and great musicality that characterised Colin's work throughout his career with the band.

At around two minutes in, the guitar and bass are united in a riff that could've come from one of the later albums if more distortion had been added: again, an early sign of the more heavy metal sound the band would later adopt.

The verse vocals sound completely resigned, reflecting the narrator's feelings of emptiness. The chorus is livelier, illustrating the relationship's fast movement from beginning to end. It could be a simple pop song chorus, as it sticks in the mind, the way that pop choruses often do. If the song stopped at three minutes, it could be a single; but another four minutes of largely instrumental music follows.

After treading water for a while before the final verse arrives, the track picks up momentum with a long guitar solo as it speeds towards the conclusion, where there is another brief moment of stasis leading into the next track.

'Up the Downstair' (9:59)

Another instrumental. According to *Stars Die*, this is a 'menacing trance epic'. After 'Voyage 34' was removed from the album, due to its length, Steven was keen to replace it with another trance track.

The song marks the introduction to the band of keyboard player Richard Barbieri: 'Steven wanted me to overlay lots of analogue electronics. I hadn't been using overly synthetic sounds for a while, so it was nice to work with pure electronic approaches.' The track also features spoken words from Richard's wife Suzanne: a writer and musician. She's sung backing vocals for various artists – including Steve Harley & Cockney Rebel, various former members of Richard's band Japan, and Jakko Jakszyk of King Crimson – and done voice-overs for several major companies. Suzanne has also written short stories and a book on the mythological and occult themes in the work of Clive Barker, whose books were the basis of the *Hellraiser* and *Candyman* horror film franchises.

The spoken words – written by Steven – are in a stream of consciousness, including phrases like 'Monuments burn into moments' (the title of an earlier short track) and 'Black Sunday of sleep/Open for small angel escapes.' The words are buried quite deep in the mix and are supposed to create a surreal impression, rather than be listened to and analysed in a conventional way.

The track begins with an ominous low drone, joined by dystopian synth lines and a Mellotron choir sounding like morose monks chanting. The synthesized bass is trancelike, euphoric and mesmeric, endlessly looping back on itself. The heavily sequenced synth chords, sparkle and glitter. The guitar part arriving in a sudden change of key around four minutes in, is urgent, driving and viscerally exciting.

At around seven minutes, the bass part drops out to a brief introspective passage, before the rhythm picks up again, tension building towards the track's climax, before dropping back into contemplation as the monks briefly return.

Being able to build up dynamics over a long track has stood Steven in good stead over his long and productive career.

'Not Beautiful Anymore' (3:26)

This title comes from a sample taken from the 1966 documentary album, *LSD*. A young woman describes the joys of taking the drug: 'You can be with somebody you like to be with, and just touch their cheek or hold their hand, and it's the most beautiful thing in the world. You don't need sex under LSD. I don't know; it's a weird trip.' Another sample says that taking LSD even replaces having children: 'I don't think that having children could make up for what I'm gonna get out of it eventually'. And the final sample confirms that having sex feels pointless and unnecessary, compared with taking LSD: 'Because you're so satisfied with just holding hands, that going for more than that, isn't beautiful anymore.'

The track feels like a coda to the previous track: 'Up the Downstair'. It has a similar bass line, although it's slower and perhaps less elegant. The track's main feature is the spoken words, for which the music stops, to ensure that they are very clear.

'Siren' (0:53)

A short, ambient instrumental with glittering synths, acting as an introduction to the next track.

'Small Fish' (Alan Duffy, Steven Wilson) (2:43)

This is a lovely, melancholy song that could've easily appeared on a psychedelic folk album in the 1960s. Allan Duffy's surreal lyric includes memorable poetic lines, such as, 'The last thing that I saw, as my life passed by/Were fields of empty people, laying down to die.'

The song seems to have an environmental theme. The 'small fish' of the title, 'gave out a cry' in response to the smile of the fishermen, implying that the fish are suffering because they're being caught. It appears the planet has reached a final apocalypse; as the narrator's life ebbs away, and the 'empty people' lie down to die, the rain lashes down in the darkness, as the sky burns and time stops.

'Burning Sky' (11:07)

Unusually for a long instrumental at this stage of Wilson's career, this track doesn't feature any spoken-word samples. The only clue to the song's meaning is the title, which takes its name from the burning sky of the previous track.

The track sounds like a whole band, even though it's all Steven's playing. Initially, he started the band so songs could be performed live, and the players brought their own musical personality. Although Steven would probably define himself as a guitarist and keyboard player, he plays excellent bass on this track: particularly at around 90 seconds in.

'Fadeaway' (Alan Duffy, Steven Wilson) (6:15)

This song remains a favourite of both Steven and Richard. Steven wrote it in the early 1980s but didn't record it with any of his earlier bands, even though he'd always thought it was 'a really beautiful song'.

It begins with the protagonist sitting in 'a room with a view': like the central character in the novel of the same name by English writer, E. M. Forster (published in 1908 and turned into a film in 1985). Although the phrase refers to a hotel room with a scenic view, in the novel, it's a metaphor for the central character – Lucy Honeychurch – trying to escape from the repressive society surrounding her. In the song, the protagonist is metaphorically and physically trapped in the room; alienated from society, climbing the walls in frustration, lost in memories of a girl from an old relationship, who now laughs at him from a photograph. The song ends in the bleak realisation that his relationships, hopes and expectations were always unrealistic; he 'hit heaven too high'. His only contact with the outside world now is in a scene – presumably imaginary – in which he becomes an object of ridicule on stage: 'I fell through a hole in the floor/The audience cried out for more.'

The track is melancholy and has a slow pace that gives a haunting quality, suiting the lyric theme well. It features Steven's fine guitar work with atmospheric synth washes. It draws strength from its simplicity, contrasting with the immensely complex but equally effective arrangements of some of the band's other songs. As with many of Steven's albums, *Up the Downstair* ends with a gentle ballad rather than an epic.

The Sky Moves Sideways (1995)

Personnel:

Steven Wilson: acoustic, electric and spiral guitars, keyboards, tapes, vocals; all sounds on original versions of 'Dislocated Day' and 'The Moon Touches Your Shoulder'

Richard Barbieri: keyboards, electronics

Colin Edwin: acoustic and electric bass

Chris Maitland: drums, percussion, hum-wah

Rick Edwards: percussion on 'Moonloop'

Suzanne J. Barbieri: vocals on 'The Sky Moves Sideways Phase 2'

Theo Travis: flute (not credited on the original 1995 release)

Gavin Harrison: drums on later versions of 'Dislocated Day' and 'The Moon Touches Your Shoulder'

Recorded at No Man's Land, June 1993 to July 1994; and the Doghouse, with the assistance of Markus Butler

Produced and mixed by Steven Wilson

Release dates: February 1995 (Delerium Records, original UK single CD version); C & S Records, original US single CD version, which included the track 'Stars Die'); November 2003 (Delerium, Remastered two-CD version)

Chart placings: Did not chart

Running time: 65:33

Record label: Delerium Records

Current release: Kscope

Porcupine Tree's third studio album is dedicated to 'Terumi and the spirit of Nick Drake'. The album marks the period when Porcupine Tree was becoming a full band. Bassist Colin Edwin, drummer Chris Maitland, and keyboard player Richard Barbieri joined Steven Wilson for the next four albums, up to and including *Lightbulb Sun* (2000). Wilson's original solo versions of 'The Moon Touches Your Shoulder' and 'Dislocated Day' having new Gavin Harrison drum parts on the 2003 album reissue, illustrate Wilson's transition from solo artist to band. Harrison had been a band member since recording 2002's *In Absentia*.

The Sky Moves Sideways was the first Porcupine Tree album to be released in America, albeit with a different tracklist, including the song 'Stars Die'. According to Wilson's website, there are three distinct versions of the album – the original UK version, the US version and the 2004 remaster – no two of which feature the same tracklist or the same version of 'Moonloop'.

The original plan was for the album to consist of the title track only, with a length of 50 minutes. The song was never completed, though an alternate version with some music cut from the final album, and an earlier set of lyrics, was released on later editions. On the band's website, Wilson said, 'As time went on, I realised that the piece was not as good as I had hoped. It was certainly one of the most derivative things I had done, and I think a lot of the Pink Floyd comparisons justifiably come from this track. So I had to split the track into two halves and recorded some shorter songs.'

Though the track was no longer the 50-minute epic it could've been, the song's two parts – or 'phases' – still rendered a 35-minute track. For the first time, the band strayed into prog rock territory: a place it found difficult to escape from in future years. Wilson takes up the story: 'Ah... the *progressive rock* album. Until this album, the progressive rock fraternity had taken very little interest in the band at all. We were considered to be more of a space-rock band, but the magnum opus title track on this put paid to that.' Rather surprisingly, Steven went on to admit on the band's website that: 'It's well known that this is not my favourite Porcupine Tree album.' This was partly because he didn't want to be seen as being derivative of another band's style, despite the joyful expectation at the time among some fans that the band would become 'the new Pink Floyd'.

I can almost guarantee that if anybody tells me this is their favourite, they will turn out to be a big Pink Floyd fan. Regardless of the quality of the execution of the material, I dislike the idea of being indebted to another band or catering for an existing audience for a definable kind of music.

Rather more revealingly and poignantly, Wilson told Stephen Humphries (in the notes for the thirteen-CD box set, *Porcupine Tree: The Delerium Years 1991-1997*, released in 2020) that he was desperate to prove he could earn a living making music. He had given up his day job and started writing music for commercials to keep some money coming in. His other band – No-Man – was not selling many records, despite initial music-press interest: 'You have to understand, at this point in time, I'm doing anything I can to get a foothold in the industry so that I can be a professional musician.'

Noting the success of the Pink Floyd-influenced song, 'Radioactive Toy' (from *On the Sunday of Life*) – which had 'gone down phenomenally well' – Wilson decided to make 'a record that I thought might do well'. Splitting the title track into two sections – album opener and closer – was another nod to Pink Floyd, who split 'Shine On You Crazy Diamond' into 'Parts I-V' and 'Parts VI-IX': opening and closing their 1975 album, *Wish You Were Here*.

In 1994 Steven told Pete Clemons of *Coventry Music Articles* blogspot: 'I wish I'd written a couple more songs to balance out the long instrumental sequences,' and that he'd never quite been able to get the title track right: 'A piece as long and complex as that one, had to be recorded in about six separate sections, and then edited together for the album. The final edit you hear on the album was about the tenth attempt to cut things to the right length and in the right order, and it's still not perfect.'

Part of the difficulty was that the recording technology Steven used then was fairly limited. Editing is easy with modern digital software, but Steven was using the ADAT format (Alesis Digital Audio Tape), which was based on VHS video tape technology, and sometimes the machine chewed up the tapes.

The album cover is an image of a traditional red English telephone box – like the Tardis from *Doctor Who* – set in a barren, rocky landscape. Claudine

Schafer took the landscape photographs in Wales, the composite image then created in an early version of Photoshop. The band's manager, Richard Allen, told Stephen Humphries that, 'It was very expensive. Looking at it now, it looks very amateurish. At the time, it was something that was quite cutting edge, because that technology had only just come through.'

The image clearly owes a debt to Hipgnosis and their Pink Floyd cover work, which combined high-quality photography and surreal imagery. The difference was that Hipgnosis had a massive budget; if they wanted an image of a huge inflatable pig flying over Battersea Power Station, they could fly an actual inflatable pig over that building, rather than just use Photoshop (although the pig on the cover of Pink Floyd's *Animals* was actually cut and pasted from another photograph, due to the weather on the day of the shoot). But perhaps more important at this stage in Porcupine Tree's career was the message the new cover sent to potential fans. Steven Wilson said: 'It was all about pushing the right buttons to attract the right kind of audience.'

Steven later said he should've used the cover for the *Moonloop* EP, which featured the track, 'Stars Die': eventually used for the compilation album *Stars Die*. That cover shows a grand piano on fire, falling from the sky towards a wooden walkway at Marsh Lock: a lock and weir situated on the River Thames near Henley-on-Thames, Oxfordshire, England. The photograph – by Mike Diver – is manipulated to look like the photo-realistic, surrealist work of Spanish artist, Salvador Dalí, and as such, has aged better than the original cover for the *Sky Moves Sideways*.

The Sky Moves Sideways is the first Porcupine Tree album for which Steven Wilson wrote all the lyrics. The first two albums included a mixture of lyrics by him and Alan Duffy. As such, this album represents an important milestone; Steven writing all the lyrics for Porcupine Tree, and his solo albums thereafter. This album's lyrics are very sparse, however. The first track, 'The Sky Moves Sideways Phase 1', includes a short section – 'I find that I'm not here' – with lyrics. Otherwise, only 'A Dislocated Day' and 'The Moon Touches Your Shoulder' – both relatively short tracks – have lyrics. In total, only about fifteen of the original UK release's 50-ish minutes include lyrics. This makes this the only almost-entirely-instrumental album Steven has produced to date, as either a solo artist or with Porcupine Tree.

The album's main concept is space. But the landscape is often emotional and metaphorical: a journey inside the central character's psyche rather than in a spaceship.

All music and lyrics by Steven Wilson, except where marked.

The Original 1995 UK CD release
'The Sky Moves Sideways Phase 1' (18:37)
According to the *Stars Die* compilation sleeve notes for this is track, Steven '...served notice on the old Porcupine Tree sound and brought in a much

lusher, pastoral-ambient sound. Probably the most single-mindedly beautiful composition in the Porcupine Tree catalogue.'

I. 'The Colour of Air'

Part 1 opens with ambient synth chords that could've come from an early Tangerine Dream album. A Mellotron choir joins, with richly ambiguous, overlapping chords.

Early in the track, there's a quote from Alan Bennett's screenplay for the Steven Frears-directed *Prick Up Your Ears* (1987). In the scene, the character, Kenneth Halliwell (played by Alfred Molina), addresses himself in the mirror before murdering the playwright, Joe Orton (played by Gary Oldman): saying that he doesn't understand his life, as he had everything he wanted as an artist.

At around a minute into the track, there's the sound of a train: evocative of Steven Wilson's childhood, as will be seen on later albums.

Slow, stately chords, measured percussion and slide guitar create a feeling of floating in space.

II. 'I Find That I'm Not There'

This is the only song section to include lyrics. It has a lovely, desolate feel, as the protagonist seems to disappear; first going off the map, before not being there at all. The lyrics are a mix of the surreal and the poetic, suggesting space travel but also a journey to inner consciousness. The vocals have a contemplative introspection – enhanced through the use of echo – and a desperate, almost angry, despairing tone. The result is one of Steven Wilson's most compelling, early vocal performances.

This section is musically strong too, with a powerful descending synth drone, and languid, bluesy guitar.

III. 'Wire the Drum'

This section takes on more urgency, with shimmering, sequenced synths, and a driving bass line, creating an almost trance-like feel. Colin Edwin's hypnotic bass switches up a minor third as squalling guitars appear above. Perhaps the best moment is when the bass drops back down to the original key, and Colin plays a characteristic looping fretless bass line: an early indication of what an asset he was to the band – his playing always subtle and uplifting.

After this frenetic dance section, a moment of respite brings a repeating flute motif (presumably played by Theo Travis, although he wasn't credited on the original album), creating a more psychedelic atmosphere, before the two styles merge.

IV. 'Spiral Circus'

The entire piece ends with another psychedelic section featuring luminous synths swirling around acoustic guitars that pivot gently between two chords.

33

The section title was also used for the band's first live album: released in limited editions, on cassette in April 1994, and vinyl in February 1997. 'Spiral Circus' itself doesn't appear on that album.

'Dislocated Day' (5:24)

On the original 1995 album, all instruments on this track and the next were performed by Steven Wilson. Gavin Harrison later added drums for the 2004 re-release.

The track begins with a phone call, which is not answered until the end, when Steven is heard leaving a message.

The track's rhythm is quite uneven and jerky, creating a physical impression of the title's dislocation: beautifully expressed through floating synthesizers and detached vocals, drifting downwards as the track progresses.

The lyrics are quite surreal – suggesting that Alan Duffy was still an influence at this point – retaining some of Alan's quirky wit: 'Stood beside an inlet/A starfish leads a dance/It dreams it is a human/And falls into a trance.'

The song ends with a recorded telephone message, in which Steven gives us a glimpse of his thoughts about how the track could end. But rather than replacing that thought with the musical action, he leaves the raw idea: '… acoustic guitar ... feeding back towards the end. I think that would make quite an interesting ending. Anyway, let me know what you think and I'll speak to you soon. Bye.'

'The Moon Touches Your Shoulder' (5:40)

This is an early example of what became a classic Porcupine Tree technique: combining various styles – such as melancholy balladry and heavy metal riffs – into one song, creating a signature sound that became, perhaps, the band's most important legacy. The original version features Wilson playing all the instruments.

The song begins with a lovely, introspective, melancholy feel, consisting largely of acoustic guitars and bluesy electric guitars for the first half. The addition of drums and lovely Floydian guitar, bring it to life, ending with a repeated guitar and bass unison riff.

The vocal melody is very simple: beginning with a rising three-note figure that immediately falls back on itself. Lush guitar chords create harmonic interest, changing key while the main vocal melody stays the same. The vocal line's simplicity matches the lyric imagery: a series of simple but apparently unrelated pictures creating meanings that feel slightly out of reach, but are poetic nonetheless: 'Springtime is over/Don't head for home/Creep up the ladder/And steal over stone.'

'Prepare Yourself' (1:58)

A short instrumental with Steven Wilson as a solo guitarist. It begins with a mournful guitar riff, soon joined by wailing, bluesy guitars.

'Moonloop' (Rick Edwards, Colin Edwin, Chris Maitland, Steven Wilson) (17:04)

If circumstances had been different, this could've been the first track featuring the full band, and also giving them a writing credit. It includes three of the four members: Wilson, Edwin and Maitland. The only person missing from the full line-up was keyboard player Richard Barbieri, who was abroad at the time. On the band's site, he described this as 'my favourite track on the album ... even though the bastards recorded it without me!'

Rick Edwards provides percussion in a 40-minute jam session recorded at Henley's Doghouse Studios: owned by Barrie 'Barriemore' Barlow – drummer with Jethro Tull in the 1970s.

Bassist, Colin Edwin, told Stephen Humphries that the band's manager, Richard Allen, was watching them as they improvised, which had the effect of concentrating their minds: 'I had this thought in my mind that it shouldn't be a self-indulgent jam – we should play something listenable. Having an audience, having somebody there, made us perhaps a bit more restrained. But it made for a more involving listen.'

Steven was inspired to record a song about the Moon, when, in an Oxfam shop, he found a vinyl copy of the spoken word recording, *Man On The Moon*, narrated by Walter Cronkite: the American broadcaster who anchored *CBS Evening News* for nearly twenty years.

The song was recorded in July 1995: 26 years after the Apollo 11 Moon landing. In July 1969 – as the Moon landing took place – Pink Floyd were in a television studio, improvising another Moon-themed piece. Floyd guitarist, David Gilmour, wrote in *The Guardian* in July 2009: 'They were broadcasting the Moon landing, and they thought that to provide a bit of a break, they would show us jamming. It was only about five minutes long. The song was called 'Moonhead' – it's a nice, atmospheric, spacey, 12-bar blues'.

The sample near 'Moonloop''s end, is a NASA recording of the Apollo 11 Astronauts, Buzz Aldrin and Neil Armstrong, at Tranquility (sic) Base on the Moon, communicating by radio with Bruce McCandless: an astronaut at Mission Control in Houston. In a heavily edited recording, Neil Armstrong can be heard climbing down the Lunar Module ladder, describing the Moon's surface as he sets foot on it. It was at this point that he made his most famous quote – which is not present in the sample – 'That's one small step for man; one giant leap for mankind'

The track begins with what could be the sound of an ocean on the Moon. Early astronomers thought the sea of tranquillity – or Mare Tranquillitatis -was actually a sea, though closer inspection revealed it to be a dry plain created by ancient volcanic eruptions.

Colin Edwin's bass part is one of the most laid-back lines (with small embellishments) he wrote for the band. Above it, Wilson's distorted guitar provides space-rock stylings until around fifteen minutes in, when the song reaches a stasis point, and the above-quoted samples appear.

The song has a trance-like, hypnotic feel, making it part of the space rock that began in the 1960s – with bands like Gong and Hawkwind – and resurfaced in the 1990s.

'The Sky Moves Sideways Phase 2' (16:46)

As did 'Phase 1', this instrumental – the opening track's second part – features all members of the band. It is divided into two sections:

I. 'Is...Not'

The track begins with ambient synths and Chris Maitland's amazing drum rolls. Synths sounding like Rick Wright's parts on Pink Floyd's 'Shine on You Crazy Diamond' follow at around three minutes in. Suddenly – at just under five minutes in – the track shakes off the ambient feel, becoming a rock instrumental with driving drums and guitars; followed by wordless vocals from Suzanne Barbieri, spacey organ and raging, distorted guitar. It's a surprising but effective transition from the early part of the song.

At around nine minutes in, a further transition leads to a more psychedelic section, with heavy percussion, in turn leading to a more spacey synth passage.

II. 'Off the Map'

The second section begins with a brief burst of Steven's backwards and deliberately unintelligible vocals, and the same stately rhythm from the opening of 'Phase 1' at the album's beginning. An extended guitar passage seems to channel David Gilmour.

The 'Moonloop' sea noises, return, with Colin Edwin's lovely upright-bass-playing accompanied by synthesized animal noises until the track fades.

'Stars Die' (5.01)

The track appears on the *Moonloop* EP released in the UK in October 1994, and was released in the US as the *Stars Die* EP with 'Moonloop' and 'Always Never' from *Up the Downstair.*

The Original 1995 US release of *The Sky Moves Sideways* included 'The Sky Moves Sideways' (Phases 1 and 2), 'Moonloop' (a must shorter version at only 8.10), 'Dislocated Day', 'The Moon Touches Your Shoulder', and 'Stars Die': which was not on the original UK album. Steven Wilson told Stephen Humphries: 'It's the strongest song that I had from that whole period,' a suggestion of the direction the band would take on future albums. It, therefore, seems strange that 'Stars Die' was left off the original UK album. He said this was partly due to his idea of having a separate EP or single of material not on an album. Perhaps he was thinking of singles like The Beatles' 1967 double A-side, 'Penny Lane' /'Strawberry Fields Forever', which didn't appear on *Sgt. Pepper's Lonely Hearts Club Band* when released a few months later.

The song is beautifully melancholy, with a simple but haunting chorus consisting of only the title, in a two-note rising phrase with luxurious backing vocals. The concept of stars dying suggests that, in the long term, everything dies; that humanity is fragile and ephemeral, and that Earth itself will eventually perish: 'Tree cracked/And mountain cried/Bridges broke/And window sighed.'

The sample at around 2:30 is of President Richard Nixon speaking from the White House Oval Office to the Apollo 11 astronauts Neil Armstrong and Buzz Aldrin when they were on the Moon. In what he describes as 'the most historic telephone call ever made', the President says the astronauts' achievements have inspired mankind to 'redouble our efforts to bring peace and tranquillity to Earth'.

Perhaps the Moon mission brought hope. But the song itself doesn't suggest peace and tranquillity will come to Earth. It ends with an image of humanity blasting away into space – astronauts in 'hyper sleep': the deep coma-like sleep that's essential for long-distance space travel. If human beings are leaving the dying Earth to seek new life elsewhere in the universe, it now seems likely that the Moon will become a jumping-off point for travel to Mars, which would make the next Moon landing even more historic.

Signify (1996)

Personnel:

Steven Wilson: vocals, electric and acoustic guitars, banshee guitar, sampler, tapes, Mellotron, organ, samples, keyboards, drum programming, piano, chimes, musical boxes

Richard Barbieri: Texture, System 700, tapes, synthesizers, Hammond organ, sequencer, Prophet-5

Colin Edwin: electric bass, double bass

Chris Maitland: drums, vocal harmonies, drum loops, cymbal

Terumi: Voices (Track one only)

Recorded at: No Man's Land, Hemel Hempstead; The Doghouse, Henley; and Katrina and the Waves' Studio, Cambridge – 1995-1996

Produced and mixed by: Steven Wilson

Release date: September 1996

Chart placings: Did not chart

Running time: 61:56

Record label: Delerium

Current release: Kscope

Signify was the first time the band were able to work together on a complete album. However, the project was still modest from a practical point of view, though not in terms of creative ambition. Most of it was recorded at No Man's Land: Steven's home studio. In July 1999, in an interview with Jerry Kranitz and Keith Henderson of *Aural Innovations* magazine, he said that *Signify* cost about £2,000 to record. To put that in context, the next album – *Stupid Dream* (1999) – cost about £15,000. By the time the band reached their seventh album – *In Absentia* (2002) – the record company provided $400,000 to cover recording costs at New York's Avatar Studios and the album's promotional tour.

It would be a mistake to assume that the album's small budget meant Steven wouldn't be able to address important aspects of human existence. Although not strictly a concept album, *Signify* does have a loose theme; although, unlike some of the later albums, the concept isn't immediately obvious from the artwork. The cover photograph – depicting a young woman suspended from ropes – appears to have been taken in the 1920s: the pinafore hemline appears to reach her knees. According to the *Women's History Network* website in September 2003, dresses reached the floor in the 'Prim and Proper Pre-1920s', briefly rising during the 'The Roaring 1920s', dropping to the floor again in 'The crashing 1930s'. The sepia tone photograph also suggests it could date back to the 1920s. But in fact, the image was taken much more recently by the graphic designer, John Blackford. Steven Wilson told Stephen Humphries in the notes for the box set *Porcupine Tree: The Delerium Years 1991-1997* that the image '...related quite well to the song 'Waiting', (which) has a slightly pervy undercurrent. The song has a line in it about waiting to be tied up. There was something that resonated just enough for me to think, 'You know what? This could be a perfect cover'.'

Humphries astutely points to other *Signify* songs in which people seek to escape from themselves in extreme ways ('Sleep of No Dreaming', Every Home Is Wired' and 'Dark Matter'). But if the album has a unifying theme, it's the existential human struggle to make something significant out of life: to create a life to signify something. Wilson told Humphries that the idea came to him while working on one of the album's early songs: 'Dark Matter.' As explained below, this track began as a fairly basic commentary on the mundane existence of life on the road for a touring musician. Steven was persuaded to give it a wider appeal, so he turned it into a song about the 'ongoing struggle most of us have, to do something significant with our time on earth'. As Steven said, human struggles with existence and the attempt to make sense of 'the gift of life' have remained a favourite theme in 'nearly every album I've made ever since'.

All music and lyrics by Steven Wilson, except where marked.

'Bornlivedie' (Steven Wilson, Richard Barbieri) (1:41)

A cheerful American radio voice invites listeners: 'Wherever you are, whether you're at home or whatever', to 'Kick your shoes off and put your feet up and lean back and uh, get yourself a cup of coffee or something, and just relax and join us in enjoying some very quiet and romantic and relaxed music for a couple of hours'. Listeners who take this seriously are likely to be disappointed; the album is far from romantic and relaxed. This is an example of the British sense of humour, which is famously built on sarcasm.

The track features the voice of a woman called Terumi (to whom the *Sky Moves Sideways* album was dedicated). The words she speaks – surrounded by Richard Barbieri's dark and atmospheric synth washes – are 'Live ... Die ... Signify': encapsulating in just three words, the album's loose theme – that there is birth, life and death, but in between, we must do something of significance.

The track has other spoken words. An American voice says, 'Your call is being transferred' – which may remind some listeners of the transatlantic phone call at the end of 'Young Lust', from Pink Floyd's 1979 album *The Wall*. There then appears to be a discussion between Wilson and Terumi: 'I'm just doing this track now, this is the introduction track ... Did you take my tape away?'. This gives insight into the recording process; in theatrical terms, this would be described as 'Breaking the fourth wall': letting the audience know that you're aware of them, and are acknowledging that something artificial is being created.

'Signify' (3:26)

Signify is an unusual Porcupine Tree album – at least in terms of the full band albums – in that more than half the tracks are instrumentals. It is appropriate then, that the title track doesn't feature vocals, although this perhaps reduces the power of the concept. This was something that Wilson would improve on when writing later albums: in which the concepts would become clearer and more cohesive.

On the band's website, Wilson said that 'Signify' was 'supposed to sound like (German electronic band) Neu! ... but the more I worked on it, and the more the other guys added their presence, the more it sounded like Rush!'. He said the track originally had a second part, which went 'into the realms of (complex) time-signature progressive metal'. Part of that second section appears on the song's live version on the 1997 album, *Coma Divine*. It also appears under the title 'Signify II', on the second disc of *Stars Die*.

The album version features a deliciously unsettling heavy metal riff, starting on a bottom E which reaches up an octave, but fails to quite get there, stopping one note short of the octave, constantly defying the listener's expectations of an interval that's easy on the ear.

The live *Coma Divine* version is faster and in an even more heavy metal style. It benefits from the extra end section, where the bass line follows the guitar line as it spirals upwards until it surprisingly (and somehow satisfyingly) starts moving in contrary motion. 'Signify II' – the second section of the original song – works well, but adding another six minutes to the title track would've perhaps made it too long.

The track sprang to life from a cover version of the Neu! song, 'Hallogallo', from their eponymous 1972 album. That band was formed when Klaus Dinger and Michael Rother left an early incarnation of Kraftwerk, and the track features a rigid 4/4 rhythm in the *motorik* style pioneered by Can drummer Jaki Liebezeit. A combined version of the two tracks – called 'Hallogallo/Signify' – appears on the Porcupine Tree *Insignificance* compilation of demos and outtakes from the *Signify* sessions (released on promotional cassette in 1997). The two tracks sit uneasily together, although it's clear how one relates to the other with their driving mechanical motorik rhythms. Also, that version of 'Signify' lacks the lovely synth line that sweeps across the main album version.

'Sleep of No Dreaming' (5:24)

Three songs and just over five minutes into the album, we hear Steven Wilson's vocals for the first time. The song title may relate to one of the most famous speeches in all of English literature: Hamlet's speech (in William Shakespeare's *Hamlet*): 'To be, or not to be, that is the question.' The speech is in the form of a soliloquy, expressing Hamlet's inner thoughts about life, death and suicide. He refers to death as sleep:

> ... To die, to sleep; to sleep: perchance to dream: ay, there's the rub;
> For in that sleep of death what dreams may come
> When we have shuffled off this mortal coil,
> Must give us pause...

The title's 'sleep of no dreaming' may be death, without the 'dreams that may come' as feared by Hamlet, who views death as an 'undiscovered country', and ponders whether it's worth continuing with the 'slings and arrows of outrageous fortune' attacking him, or risking what death may bring. The concept perfectly matches the album's theme: the questioning of the nature and significance of existence.

At times – despite being the Prince of Denmark and a mature adult – Hamlet behaves more like a moody adolescent. The character in the song seems to share Hamlet's ability to consider the deeper questions of the universe while suffering from adolescent disillusionment about the world: 'At the age of sixteen/I grew out of hope/I regarded the cosmos/Through a circle of rope.' The 'circle of rope' seems to be a noose in the rope that the central character might use to take his own life; it colours everything he sees, even his deepest thoughts about the universe.

The song title could also refer to the protagonist's failure to do anything significant with his life. The track describes his complete loss of hope – his abandoning of his childish dreams, to run 'on to the wheel', to embrace a lucrative career which has destroyed his soul – so that he might as well be dead: 'Made a good living/By dying it's true.' There's a darkly comic element to the deadpan and almost resigned way Wilson delivers some of the protagonist's lines: 'I married the first girl/Who wasn't a man.'

Colin Edwin's double-bass line seems to add to the song's introspective intensity, which Richard Barbieri's atmospheric keyboards, enhance. Chris Maitland's excitable drumming gives the song a forward momentum it would otherwise lack.

'Pagan' (1:34)

This short instrumental is a companion to the album's penultimate track: 'Light Mass Prayers', a ghostly song made up of synth washes and samples, with no bass or drums. It could be from a horror movie soundtrack, with its haunting high voice endlessly repeating the motif, as if somehow trapped in another dimension.

'Waiting (Phase One)' (4:24)

This song was released as a single but didn't chart. After the lengthy 'Voyage 34' single, which was over 30 minutes long, the running time is much more normal. The track begins with the protagonist waiting to be 'born again': perhaps hoping for redemption, or at least for life to have some meaning. The repeated line, 'Waiting... for the day when I will crawl away', suggests hopelessness – even a desire for death.

As mentioned above, Steven felt the song had 'a slightly pervy undercurrent', and this is fairly explicit in the lines, 'Waiting... to be disciplined/Aching... for your nails across my skin.'

According to the *Stars Die* sleeve notes, drummer, Chris Maitland, loved singing the vocal harmonies on this song; but if forced to take only one of the tracks to a desert island, he would choose Colin Edwin's bass line, because 'It's so hypnotic and subtle'. Wilson's guitar-playing is another highlight: beginning with gentle acoustic chords, and spacey, psychedelic electric guitar, exploding towards the end in a manic solo that seems to express the protagonist's frustration.

'Waiting (Phase Two)' (6:15)

The song's second part is another instrumental, looking back in style to the previous albums, but pointing toward the transition from psychedelia to a rock and pop style – which, much later, incorporated heavy metal too.

It follows on from the previous track, with a long ambiguous string chord, guitar wailings, heavy percussion, and a psychedelic soundscape which could refer to the drugs of 'Phase One' making things 'real'. Colin Edwin's superb bassline returns, with a lovely, simple piano motif above it.

The track has an almost trippy, hypnotic feel, until it breaks down briefly, giving drummer Chris Maitland time to assert his robust presence. The track builds to a climax with Steven's searching guitar solo, until again it breaks down, with the ambiguous string chord lurking, until the song descends into noise, and breaks up altogether.

'Sever' (5:30)

In the *Stars Die* notes, Steven Wilson describes this as a 'soupy' track; meaning that all the sounds are 'crammed together'. This could also apply to the lyrics, which use the cut-up technique: putting apparently unrelated words and phrases together, to create new lyrics, and hopefully new meanings. It certainly creates a disturbing and surreal atmosphere, for what Steven described as 'perhaps the most dramatic track' on the album.

David Bowie used the cut-up technique for some of his lyrics, and although it's apparently completely random, both songwriters exercised some degree of artistic control by choosing which words actually went into their songs and in what order. The 'Sever' images are often highly resonant. For example, 'stage fright, black light, coma divine': which could suggest a musician collapsing before going on stage. But it would probably be a mistake to attempt a literal interpretation of each line; it's better to let the images float around the consciousness. The phrase 'coma divine', obviously stuck in Steven's mind, as he used it to name the live album recorded in Rome in 1997.

The song begins with a viciously menacing distorted guitar chord based on C, with heavy bass and drums. The first vocal note is F#, which, set against the note C, is an interval of a tritone or augmented 4th: regarded as a disturbing interval in Western music. This interval immediately creates a sense of unease. This is increased by the disjointed, unsettling effect from dividing the verse words up into very short separate sections so that, in some cases, individual words are split up.

The chorus features Chris Maitland's gorgeous, multitracked backing vocals: Steven was able to find beauty in the midst of the track's horror.

The song is unusual for Porcupine Tree in that the verse sits entirely on one chord. But the above-mentioned tritone shatters any sense of contentment the familiar and unchanging chord creates. Later in the song, a wordless vocal repeats the F#, adding the G a semitone above. This motif begins to dominate, taking on a frightening life of its own, as the remaining instruments fall away.

The song ends with a sample of a terrifyingly-passionate preacher shouting 'Hallelujah, Hallelujah, Hallelujah... that's the only way to survive, is on your knees', interspersed with maniacal laughter.

The track gives an insight into Steven's way of working with his band members and his role as the main songwriter. On the band's website, Colin Edwin said that it 'really only works with the specific bass line Steven had already written so that sometimes I replace the original demo parts with my own take.' This also applies to the track 'Dark Matter'. However, the end of 'Every Home Is Wired', is a double-bass solo played by Colin, with 'various treatments administered by Doctor Wilson'.

'Idiot Prayer' (Steven Wilson, Colin Edwin) (7:37)

Another instrumental track. But like the earlier 'Voyage 34', released in 1992, spoken-word samples provide a theme. We hear a sample of someone appearing to be on a drug trip which at first seems to be going well: 'I'm having the most perfect hallucination. Green and blue patterns are forming all over me like a deck of cards.' However, like Brian's trip in 'Voyage 34', the experience suddenly becomes devastating: 'I don't feel I'll ever be the same again. Please help... please help'.

Like 'Voyage 34', the track again illustrates Steven's ability to build up a long instrumental using very simple elements; although, of course, 'Idiot Prayer' is much shorter. Steven's an expert in building drama and intensity in a long-form composition: a good example being the gradual build-up to the pulsating bassline, which appears at 2:30. The bass drops out at around four minutes in; and at around five minutes, the drums – which provided a steady dance rhythm – drop out as well, leading to a wistful psychedelic section. When the drums creep back in at around 5:30, they sound like a heartbeat: perhaps the protagonist's heartbeat, as he reappears at this point, asking for help. Then at around six minutes in – with a sound like paper tearing – the bass line reappears, along with the looping guitar part that's so characteristic of the track.

Using very simple, repetitive elements, the track has a light and shade, which keeps it dynamic and vital throughout. The song is also harmonically simple, relying on an effective switching from the guitar's long-held A to the A# a semitone above, which are implicit in the harmony, even when the notes are not in the foreground. This very basic interval becomes an earworm.

'Every Home Is Wired' (5:08)

This is the first song Steven wrote about the internet and the damaging effect it could have on society: a theme he returned to a number of times over the next 25 years. In particular, it formed part of the concept behind *Fear of a Blank Planet* (2007), an album about teenage alienation caused partly by the internet. The following lines from 'Every Home Is Wired' could've easily come from the later album: 'Modem load and failsafe/Electric teenage dust/Start the neural rust ... Surfing on the network/Part of me is dead.'

As Steven correctly predicted in 1996, a world in which every home was wired up to the internet was 'the future'. According to the UK Office for National Statistics in August 2020, 'In January to February 2020, 96% of households in Great Britain had internet access: up from 93% in 2019, and 57% in 2006 when comparable records began'. In 2015, Steven wrote another album about the internet's detrimental effect on society: his solo album, *Hand. Cannot. Erase.* The concept was based on the tragic story of Joyce Carol Vincent, who died alone in her London flat in 2003, aged 38, but whose body was not found until 2006. She had cut herself off from society, despite living in one of the world's busiest cities. Steven took this idea and developed a character who only communicated with the world via her blog, which was printed out as part of the album's deluxe box set. In an interview with Lilen Pautasso of *Reverb Online* in August 2016, Steven said that since he'd written 'Every Home Is Wired', things had gotten worse and technology was not necessarily affecting the human race in a positive way. He said, 'I think for the very first time in history, the human race is in a state of devolution, going backwards, getting more stupid, and I wonder if technology can't be blamed for why that is the case...'

This message is communicated through a lovely, straightforward pop song, which, according to the *Stars Die* notes, features 'one of Steven's most ambitious vocal experiments in Beach Boys fashion – a nod from one Wilson to another ... the song layers up 37 sets of vocal overdubs to create the falling, melancholy chorus'.

The song ends with a double-bass solo from Colin Edwin.

'Intermediate Jesus' (Steven Wilson, Richard Barbieri, Colin Edwin, Chris Maitland) (7:29)

Another instrumental. According to Wilson's website, the band were unable to record together due to space limitations in No Man's Land: his home studio. This track is an exception, in that all the band members were together, outside the studio. The opening preacher's voice warns: 'With this Satanic invasion from legion diabolic, you need Christ.' The source of the sample, and the possible identity of the preacher, have been discussed on several online forums, but it appears nobody has found the exact text anywhere, and the preacher is not credited in the album sleeve notes. On the band site, Colin Edwin said the samples were so apt that they 'could have been made for the track', and dryly commented, 'perhaps we should find him and give him some royalties'.

The track has a kind of loose, psychedelic, spacey, live improvisation feel, barely exhibited elsewhere on the record: partly due to the studio's physical constraints, and because of Steven's way of working, as described on his site: 'I tended to demo the tracks to a fairly high level, and they would just replace the parts that I'd played on synthesizers, with the real thing. So there wasn't a great deal of input from the other guys.'

'Light Mass Prayers' (Chris Maitland) (4:28)

As Stephen Humphries notes, drummer Chris Maitland has 'the distinction of writing the only Porcupine Tree song not to have Wilson credit'.

On the band's site, Wilson said this song's title 'comes from words that were written on a wall at Borley Rectory (the most haunted place in England) by an unknown hand'. The Rectory was built in the parish of Borley in northeast Essex, England, in 1862. In 1939, it was badly fire-damaged and was eventually demolished in 1944. Psychic researcher Harry Price gave the description – 'The most haunted house in England' – in a 1929 *Daily Mirror* article. In 2003, local historian, Andrew Clarke, wrote a fascinating article titled *No Hand was Visible: The Wall Writings at Borley Rectory* on the Foxearth and District Local History Society website. Apparently, the rector told medium, Guy L'Estrange, that 'he was working alone in his study when he saw a pencil rise from the desk and scrawl words on the wall in front of him – no hand was visible!' Andrew Clarke outlines the words written on the wall:

> The repeated calling of Marianne's name, their chilling pleas for 'Rest', exhortations for 'Light Mass Prayers', and pathetic scribbling, redolent of a tortured soul desperate to communicate. Who can fail to be stirred by the account of their arrival as remembered by a visitor, the professional medium, Guy L'Estrange...?

But, Clarke continues, 'Unfortunately, Guy seems to have made it up.' It would be a pity to let the truth get in the way of a good story, and when Chris Maitland came to Steven Wilson with 'some chords that sounded spooky', they layered the sounds to create 'a completely drum-less, ambient instrumental'. The track features the drummer's wordless vocals, beautifully multitracked to create the sound of a choir singing in one of the Cambridge University colleges. Chris told Stephen Humphries: 'I grew up on all that Cambridge choral stuff. I still love choirs. I like the way that track faded out, as if it was disappearing into the distance.' The imagery of choral evensong in a Cambridge college chapel on a misty November afternoon, and ghostly writings on a rectory wall, seem to sit together well in the mind's eye.

The *TV Tropes* website refers to the song being an example of using 'The drone of dread':

> In music, a drone is a sustained, continuous sound, note or tone cluster. Music based around drones will emphasize minimalism and texture, timbre, eventually harmony, with less concern over rhythm and melody.

'Dark Matter' (8:52)

The final track was originally called 'Toursong'. According to the *Stars Die* notes, this song began life as 'a fairly drab account of life on the road and its attendant boredoms'. But Richard Allen and the band objected to the lyrics, which amounted to, 'came off stage, had a cup of tea, went to bed'. So Steven changed them to being 'about the business of being a musician and a product', making it 'one of the most haunting songs in the Porcupine Tree catalogue'. Steven expressed the musicians' frustration with spending 95 per cent of life as a touring artist, having no time to create something of significance: again relating to the album title.

The song title refers to the recordings which record companies regard as product, something ephemeral rather than of lasting artistic significance – a theme to which Steven returned on the next album: *Stupid Dream.*

The song begins with darkly atmospheric synth washes, forming an image of the inner tour bus permafrost: 'Inside the vehicle the cold is extreme'. Cold has become a metaphor for failure to engage with the outside world: 'I fail to connect, it's a tragic divide.'

The protagonist ruminates on the fact that music has become a full-time career, but that there are other, quicker ways, to become famous when you're young: 'To die young would take only 21 years/Gun down a school or blow up a car/The media circus would make you a star.'

The song features Richard Barbieri's gorgeous Hammond organ-playing. In the verses, Steven's voice is close-mic'd, giving the impression of the listener being on the tour bus with him. Most unusually, the verses feature backing vocals – presumably from Chris Maitland (though he's not given a specific credit). Usually, the lush vocal harmonies so characteristic of many Porcupine Tree songs appear only in the choruses; although the chorus also does feature-rich harmonies.

An extended guitar solo lasting around two minutes culminates in a short section where bass and guitar riff in unison. It's not as heavy as on the later albums but is perhaps a taster of the heavier, riff-driven style.

After the ending – at 8:10 – nineteen seconds of silence precede a hidden track, in which a cheerful American voice announces, 'You've just had a heavy session of electroshock therapy, and you're more relaxed than you've been in weeks. All those childhood traumas magically wiped away, along with most of your personality'. The same sample was used on the track 'Meat 'N Veg' on The Orb's 1994 album, *Pomme Fritz.* The sample is from a 1975 episode of the American TV show, *Saturday Night Live,* in which show announcer, Bill Wendell, voices a spoof commercial for 'Spud Beer'.

The album's closing words contrast with the opening words, which invited listeners to enjoy a couple of hours of 'very quiet and romantic and relaxed music'.

Stupid Dream (1999)

Personnel:
Steven Wilson: vocals, guitars, piano, samples, bass
Richard Barbieri: analogue synthesizers, Hammond organ, Mellotron, piano, glockenspiel
Colin Edwin: bass, double bass
Chris Maitland: drums, percussion, backing vocals
Theo Travis: flute, saxophone
East of England Orchestra conducted by Nicholas Kok: strings
Recorded at Foel Studios, Llanfair Caereinion, Wales; No Man's Land, Hemel Hempstead, England, Jan-Nov 1998; strings recorded by Chris Thorpe at Cedar Arts Centre, Derby, England
Produced and mixed by Steven Wilson at No Man's Land
Release date: UK: March 22 1999, Worldwide: April 6 1999
Chart placings: Did not chart
Running time: 59:55
Record label: Kscope

Stupid Dream is the fifth Porcupine Tree studio album. Fans of Steven Wilson's solo albums will be aware of the storm that raged around his apparent change of musical direction from the prog of *Hand. Cannot. Erase.* (2015) to the more straightforward pop of *To the Bone* (2017). *Prog* magazine even put him on the cover in August 2017, posing the question: 'Steven Wilson: Has he ditched prog for pop?'. On the bottom-left of the cover, a small disclaimer said 'No he hasn't'.

When Porcupine Tree released *Stupid Dream* nearly 20 years earlier, Steven was also then accused of moving from prog towards more song-orientated territory; communicating with lyrics in shorter pop songs rather than long-form instrumentals. In July 1999, in an interview with Jerry Kranitz and Keith Henderson of *Aural Innovations* magazine), his response was telling: 'It is not as simple as that. Every album Porcupine Tree has made has been very distinct from those that preceded it.'

The fact that Steven's always tried to not repeat himself – constantly changing style – has sometimes perplexed fans but has also been a fascinating journey. He's often said that the music he's listening to strongly influences the writing of an album. His tastes are eclectic; ever-changing and developing. He told *Aural Innovations*, 'I have a massive musical taste'. Sometimes the music he's remixing or remastering for other bands has had an influence on him: when working on *To the Bone*, he was also remixing Tears for Fears, and he acknowledged the influence of progressive pop written by that group, Peter Gabriel and Kate Bush.

But as he said on the band's site, the new musical direction of *Stupid Dream* failed to convince some prog rock fans: 'It would be only a slight exaggeration to say I was getting hate mail from some of the older fans....' He said it was a myth that most experimental music had come from the progressive field, with its long, extended pieces. Talking to *Aural Innovations* magazine, he cited The Beatles' 'Tomorrow Never Knows' from *Revolver* (1966) and The Beach Boys' 'God Only Knows' from *Pet Sounds* (1966) as examples of 'the pinnacle of popular music ... the pop song as an experimental symphony'. These songs are only about three minutes long; they are perfect miniatures. The other point is that Steven's always carefully considered the track sequencing of Porcupine Tree albums and his solo works; the shorter *Stupid Dream* pop songs form part of a more coherent whole.

So, what's the concept behind *Stupid Dream*? One of the major themes is the age-old contradiction between art and commerce. Andy Warhol once said, 'Making money is art, and working is art, and good business is the best art'; but at the time of making *Stupid Dream*, Steven would've profoundly disagreed. The album reflects his need to preserve the purity of his artistic vision, the difficulty of making art without compromise, and his cynicism about the music business.

The cover art shows a figure wearing the kind of protective clothing worn in manufacturing and laboratory clean rooms, holding up a CD obliterating the face of the person holding it. The original album cover had an electric-blue image of a person in a CD manufacturing environment, again wearing protective gear. Both images suggest music has become a shiny *product* manufactured in an environment both physically and metaphorically sterile; creativity reduced to the number of units sold. Steven spoke passionately to *Aural Innovations* about this dichotomy, about the difficulty in moving from being an artist creating music, to a businessman promoting it.

Steven's relationship to his physical product has always been ambiguous, as has his relationship to success. Sometimes he's spoken of frustration with his lack of mainstream success. But at the same time, he values the independence and integrity of his artistic vision. In terms of the physical product that fans buy, he's increasingly made them to be works of art in themselves: the 2020 CD reissue of 2002's *In Absentia* – three CDs and a DVD in an LP-sized booklet – could grace any coffee table (were it not for the horror of the cover image's eyeless man). Steven gently mocked himself in his 2020 song 'Personal Shopper' by listing 'deluxe edition box sets' along with Organic LED television and monogrammed luggage as some of the pointless items the modern consumer feels compelled to buy. But the truth is, he is providing something for fans to treasure.

The album title reflects Steven's view on the teenage dreams of being a musician. David Bowie's Ziggy Stardust said, 'I could fall asleep at night as a rock and roll star'; but this idea is obviously something that has *kept* Steven awake at night. As he said on his website, he learned that being a professional musician 'can be very heartbreaking: there's a lot of disappointment, there's a lot of hard work, there's a lot of travelling'. The assumption that fame and fortune make life wonderful, is a long way from the reality.

The album marks the first time the band worked on song arrangements as a group. Although Steven did most of the work at his home studio, over a period of ten months, the band did spend an extended period working at Foel Studios in Llanfair Caereinion, Wales: owned by bassist Dave Anderson, who'd played with Hawkwind and Amon Duul II. It's about 30 miles west of Bron-Yr-Aur, where parts of *Led Zeppelin III* were recorded.

All music and lyrics by Steven Wilson, except where marked.

'Even Less' (7:11)

The song begins with a single held A on the strings. Slide guitars evoke a sunlit, humid, American desert landscape, sounding similar to Ry Cooder's 1984 movie soundtrack, *Paris, Texas*. The guitars are doubled across the stereo channels: a technique used extensively on later Porcupine Tree albums – particularly on heavy metal guitars – to add richness and bite.

But the setting swiftly moves to an English landscape, as the chords move from slide guitar to elemental distorted chords: almost punk-like in their simplicity. Acoustic guitar and piano accompany the description of a body being washed up on a Norfolk beach; and a friend who 'could not be reached', who's presumably committed suicide.

There follows an even more disturbing image of another body, 'a choirboy buried on the moor', recalling the infamous 1960s Moors Murders: when children's bodies were disposed of on Saddleworth Moor in North West England. Another infamous murder – that of James Bulger – features in 'This Is No Rehearsal' later on the album.

The song ends in a series of heavy guitar chords in drop-D tuning, where the bottom note of the guitar is tuned down by a whole note: a technique beloved of heavy metal bands and used extensively on later Porcupine Tree albums. As such, the song marks an important transition for the band: from earlier psychedelia to later progressive metal. But Steven shows he's not moved away from psychedelia yet: above the brutal, visceral heavy metal crunch, floats a lovely Floydian guitar solo.

As the music gradually fades into nothingness, a female voice can be heard reciting a series of mysterious numbers. Steven told Ed Sander of *DPRP.net* in December 1999, that the recording was taken from shortwave radio: possibly coded messages for overseas security operatives from government security agencies. Although, as Steven said, 'They are virtually impossible to decode without the key, since the message and its key are generated at random'.

'Even Less' was originally seventeen minutes long and had a huge number of overdubs. When mixing it, Steven decided that less is more, removing ten minutes of music. He also made the mix more sparse. When questioned about this at the time, he made a perceptive comment on something that's regularly caused him difficulty, if not irritation: the perception of Porcupine Tree's music as being progressive rock. He told *Aural Innovations*: 'Porcupine Tree music is very, very simple. There's nothing complex about it all. The complexity is in the production ... I think what leads people to give it that kind of progressive tag is the way the songs are produced'.

A fourteen-minute version of the song is on the 2001 compilation, *Recordings*: the first part is the *Stupid Dream* version, and the second (only) appeared on the 'Stranger by the Minute' CD single. Steven was right to drop it from the album version; it begins well with a typical Colin Edwin bass line, but morphs into an extended jam that would work well in a live situation but does so less well as an album's opening track.

'Piano Lessons' (4:21)

Released as a single that did not chart.

Jaunty is not a word that would normally be used to describe a Porcupine Tree track, but this piano-led psychedelic pop song could be described in that way. It could easily be a Beatles song, and the chorus could be from a Tears for Fears song, although the guitar line swooping above, gives a more psychedelic feel.

The album's theme of bitter sarcasm towards the music industry comes across clearly, and even more so in the music video. Filmed in a quirky, almost comedic style – like a silent movie – it features characters holding up cards that say things like, 'promotional video', 'subliminal message', 'buy', 'product' and (helpfully) 'guitar solo'. In places, the style is reminiscent of the promotional film for Pink Floyd's 1967 single, 'Arnold Layne', which also looks like a silent film, and shows Roger Waters in a frock coat, similar to the coat Steven is briefly seen wearing over 30 years later. Both videos are pastiches, and both songs also hide a darker secret behind their surface of 1960s high-spirited jollity.

The 'Piano Lessons' video was directed by Mike Bennion: later Steven's collaborator on the *Deadwing* project. Mike is a director of TV ads, for which Steven has written a lot of music: 'I'm not about to tell you which ones', he said in the 1999 *Aural Innovations* interview. Writing music for TV commercials was still Steven's main earner: 'It pays very well and means I can do what the hell I like the rest of the year'. Most of the Porcupine Tree money was still being ploughed back into the band. The other members also had to supplement their income. Chris Maitland and Colin Edwin made money from instrument tuition, and Richard Barbieri had other projects and a record label.

'Stupid Dream' (0:28)

The title track is very unusual. Instead of the rant against the music industry you might expect, it's an instrumental and under 30 seconds long. It begins like an opera, heard through the layers of a dream: a montage of a soprano singing an opera aria and the sound of orchestral strings, tuning. The aria is part of 'Vissi d'arte, Vissi d'amore', from Act II of Italian composer, Puccini's opera, *Tosca*. The opening words translate as, 'I lived for my art', which seems appropriate in light of the album's theme: the dichotomy between art and commerce.

'Pure Narcotic' (5:02)

Released as a single that did not chart.

This is the first of a trio of songs about unrequited love, which become more rancorous as the mini song cycle continues. Though the track's sentiment is bitter, the tone is contemplative rather than angry; resigned rather than relentless. The vocals are gentle, sung in a gorgeous, folk-ish style, with a charming folk arrangement featuring acoustic guitars, piano, tender harmonies, and Richard Barbieri on glockenspiel.

The object of the writer's unrequited love forces him to listen to Radiohead's second album *The Bends* (1995). But rather than the muscular rock of *The Bends*, 'Pure Narcotic' feels closer in style to later Radiohead songs, like 'How To Disappear Completely': a gentle song about existential despair, led by acoustic guitars and floating strings. The beautiful chorus of 'Pure Narcotic' consists of ambiguous alternating major and minor chords, creating a feeling of gentle nostalgia.

The song ends with probably one of Wilson's favourite images – that of the railway: 'Leave me dreaming on a railway track.' Generally, the imagery is associated with his nostalgia for childhood, as in the song, 'Trains', from *In Absentia* (2002). Steven has said that he rarely travels by train, preferring to use his car, so the nostalgic train travel memory remains preserved in aspic for him.

'Slave Called Shiver' (4:40)

The second of the trio of songs about unrequited love; much more disturbing than the last. It starts with Colin Edwin's characteristically funky, looping bass line. The drums sound as if recorded in a very good 'live' room. The piano part has a similar feel to the bass, but before you get too comfortable, it's made unsettling by alternately switching between the major and minor key. The vocals are heavily compressed: often a sign in Porcupine Tree music that the subject matter is very dark. Steven's voice sounds both intimate and sinister – the compression adding urgency to the vocal delivery. The guitar line sounds as if it's recorded backwards – using a technique pioneered by The Beatles in songs like 'I'm Only Sleeping' (1966) – adding to the general sense of unease.

The object of desire is viewed from a distance, and what could be a tender opening line – 'I need you more than you can know' – becomes distorted by the next line: 'And if I hurt myself it's just for show'. The 'pure narcotic' effect on the previous song's unrequited lover, has now become a 'trigger' inside his brain. The protagonist menacingly threatens that, although he is nothing now, 'I'll have more followers than Jesus Christ'.

The song ends with a driving guitar/bass unison riff, foreshadowing the heavier progressive metal style of *In Absentia* (2002).

'Don't Hate Me' (8:30)

The final song in the trilogy begins with an image of a deserted London, as light snow falls. But for once, the image of a train doesn't represent Steven's childhood nostalgia, but the emptiness of the scene, as no one gets on or off the train. The relationship has broken up, and a sense of weary resignation haunts the song's verses. The chorus is more impassioned, as the unrequited lover – who's so 'tired and alone' – pleads not to be hated: a plea moderated by the deeply sarcastic line, 'I'm not special like you'.

This is one of Porcupine Tree's most atmospheric songs, with a jazz-inflected interlude, switching between a laid-back flute solo and a more anguished saxophone – both played by Theo Travis – moving from resignation to bitter anger. The long interlude would perfectly suit a noir movie, as it evokes dark streets with silhouetted figures and cigarette smoke curling through darkened rooms. Steven has often spoken of his songs being like short films, and this is a perfect example.

A newer version of the song is on Wilson's 2016 solo mini-album, *4 ½*. This time it's sung as a duet with the Israeli singer, Ninet Tayeb, who'd featured most memorably on 'Routine' from *Hand. Cannot. Erase* (2015). The song, as a duet, makes the contrast between verse and chorus even clearer. Ninet's rich mezzo-soprano is an inspired choice. She sings in the same octave as Steven does on the original version: as high in his range as it is low in Ninet's; making her intense chorus vocal more sultry, but equally passionate.

It's fascinating to compare the instrumental performances in the two different versions. The *4 ½* version is taken from a live recording made on Steven's 2015 European tour and features Craig Blundell on drums, Adam Holzman on keyboards, and Nick Beggs on bass. Theo Travis plays flute on the Porcupine Tree version and saxophone on both.

In the jazzy interlude, the later version features the quicksilver keyboards of Adam Holzman, compared with Theo Travis' mournful, lonely flute of the original. In some ways, the contrast between bass players is the most interesting. Edwin's playing is loose and syncopated, with a warm tone. Nick Beggs' is more focused in tone, angular and tightly rhythmic. Both are amazing.

'This Is No Rehearsal' (3:26)

This song is based on the horrifying case of James Bulger: a two-year-old boy, who in 1993 was abducted from a shopping centre in Bootle, Merseyside, and brutally murdered. Even more shocking was that his murderers – Jon Venables and Robert Thompson – were only ten years old at the time. James' mother was briefly distracted and didn't notice that the boys had taken her son; the CCTV image of one of the boys holding the toddler's hand as they walked through the shopping centre, is etched deep into England's national psyche, showing the little boy's trust as he held the hand of a boy not much older than him, who was leading him to his brutal death. The case raised profound questions about the nature of justice (the boys were tried as adults) and the provision of anonymity to the boys when they became adults.

Steven's poignant lyric goes right to the heart of the mother's tragedy; the tenderness of the relationship with her son, and his young age, expressed by the fact that she was still dressing him on the day he died: 'And still I remember how I dressed him this morning/And then he was gone – stolen, my only one.'

The almost choirboy-like purity of Steven's vocal delivery – suggesting a mother's despair – contrasts with the almost funky instrumental parts. This contrast is an example of the cognitive dissonance lying at the heart of many of Porcupine Tree's songs. A cursory listen to what appears to be a straightforward pop song does not reveal the true meaning.

James Bulger's body was found on a railway track; in harrowing and ironic contrast to Steven's association of railways with childhood nostalgia.

'Baby Dream in Cellophane' (3:15)

An initial reaction to this song could be that the title refers to a 'plain wrapper baby': the inflatable doll featuring so memorably in Roxy Music's 'In Every Dream Home a Heartache' (from *For Your Pleasure*, 1973). That song could've easily been on a Porcupine Tree album, such as *In Absentia* with its dark tales of serial killers.

But in fact, this song is about a baby in a pram, although the baby is not viewed in a sentimental or nostalgic way. It's a surreal song about a baby who refuses to follow the life plan society has predetermined for him. As Steven told *DPRP.net*: 'If you imagine Nirvana if they wrote about rebellious teenagers, I write songs for rebellious babies'.

The track begins with anxious acoustic guitars and heavily compressed vocals. The minor-key tension suddenly releases through modulation to the major, and a bridge passage leads to a gorgeous explosion of harmony vocals in the chorus. This reflects Steven's passion for the rich vocal harmonies of The Beach Boys and Crosby, Stills, Nash & Young. There's also a thematic and musical link with Pink Floyd's 'Goodbye Blue Sky' from *The Wall* (1979): both songs heavily feature acoustic guitars and radiant vocal harmonies, and both are about the loss of childhood innocence.

'Stranger by the Minute' (4:30)

Released as a single that did not chart.

The single's promotional version had a sticker attached, proudly proclaiming, 'It combines billowing harmonies with hauntingly-stark yet fascinatingly-warm melodies'. For once, the hype was accurate.

The single cover image shows a person in a protective suit, in a cornfield, holding what appears to be a Geiger counter (see the commentary on 'A Smart Kid' below).

Lyrically, the song gets Stranger by the Minute, as surreal and dreamlike images pile up on top of each other. Musically, the song is simple: shot-through with sunlight, in a rare moment of joy for a Porcupine Tree record. It's indie rock, with an evocative guitar slide from chord to chord and a lovely, bluesy guitar solo.

'A Smart Kid' (5:22)

A quietly melancholy song about the infinite loneliness suffered by the protagonist: the last remaining human being, stranded on planet Earth, after what seems to have been a five-year nuclear winter. After 'a chemical harvest was sown', nuclear clouds obscure the sun. It seems there was a nuclear war, which the protagonist 'must have won': making the song title profoundly ironic. He has won an empty victory.

The nuclear war theme relates to 'Radioactive Toy' (from 1992's *On the Sunday of Life*), in which the 'toy' gives 'the freedom to destroy'. It would perhaps be foolish to describe Robert Oppenheimer – credited as the 'father of the atomic bomb' – as merely a 'smart kid' like the song's protagonist. The reality is much more subtle, but Oppenheimer did later express regret about the 'sin' that he and other physicists had committed: that once the knowledge that created the atomic bomb had been gained, it could never be lost again.

The theme of Earth's destruction is also explored in 'Last Chance to Evacuate Planet Earth Before It Is Recycled' on the next album, *Lightbulb Sun* (2000).

In 'A Smart Kid', the protagonist is waiting for an alien spaceship to arrive to rescue him from Earth. He will wait 'until the sky is blue'. The implication is that it will never be blue again.

The song is rich in metaphor, which has led to some fascinating interpretations on various online forums. One suggestion is that the five long years refers to the Holocaust, and that the chemical harvest refers to the gas chambers. Another is that the song is about depression, and the long wait for the sun to rise again refers to the lifting of depression.

Perhaps the most interesting interpretation comes from Brice Ezell on the *PopMatters* website in May 2012, where the lines 'Everything's free here/ There's no crowd' are seen as part of the album's 'consumerist critique'. The only way to deal with an 'increasingly commodified world' is to destroy it. The irony is that the freedom to destroy the hyper-capitalist system and the greedy music industry – the targets of the album's critique – is the freedom to destroy the world – a very elegant explanation.

The song begins with a short A chord on orchestral strings, like an orchestra tuning up, creating anticipation at the start of a concert. Beautifully-recorded acoustic guitars – tranquil and lonely – make the repeated orchestral A chord now sound ambiguous, as if no longer belonging in the song. Heavily-echoed synthesizer notes add to the feeling of isolation.

Wilson's vocal performance adds to the sense of desolation. The verses are sweetly sung; the heavily compressed chorus vocals, giving an impression of distancing and alienation.

The atmospheric middle eight (played twice) features the sound of a Geiger counter spluttering away in reaction to toxic nuclear radiation. The soundscape – including close-mic'd breathing inside a protective suit – is similar to that of Wilson's early solo albums: particularly *Insurgentes* (2008). Appropriately enough, on that album's cover, Steven is wearing a gas mask, which he also took to wearing on the record's promotional tour.

'Tinto Brass' (Richard Barbieri, Colin Edwin, Chris Maitland, Steven Wilson) (6:17)

The only song here written by the band as a whole sounds like a joyous jam; although it starts ominously enough, with a brief burst of dense textures not unlike *Atmosphères*: by Hungarian-Austrian composer, György Ligeti. Director, Stanley Kubrick, used the piece in *2001: A Space Odyssey* (1968). (Kubrick is one of Wilson's favourite directors). Tinto Brass is also a film director (Italian), most famous for his involvement with the 1979 movie *Caligula*. Brass had his name removed from the credits when the studio turned Gore Vidal's screenplay (originally a political satire) into what was effectively a porn film. Perhaps Brass should've been forewarned that the film's producer was Bob Guccione: founder of *Penthouse* magazine. Steven had seen Brass' name on the cover of a video, but was unable to find any Brass information written in English.

The track begins with Terumi reading a short Brass biography in Japanese. The track marks a brief return to the more psychedelic style of the earlier Porcupine Tree, with the jazz-like flute of Theo Travis, a funky bass line and heavy echo. A restlessly busy track, it's constantly uplifting as it twists and turns, even toying briefly – but dangerously – with some heavy metal riffs.

Steven chose the name of another film director, Harmony Korine, for the opening song title on his first solo album, *Insurgentes* (2008).

'Stop Swimming' (6:53)

This song is about Steven's relationship with the music industry and his occasional strong impulse to stop swimming; to give up and just go with the flow. This is partly due to the frustration he feels with his lack of commercial success.

Shot through with melancholy, the opening piano chords feature a lovely change from major to minor: a technique beloved of The Beatles; and also Cole Porter, who famously found this modulation 'strange' in his 'Ev'ry Time We Say Goodbye'. Steven's vocal is resigned, and the song seeps gently into the consciousness, 'Leaking out onto the pavement', as the opening line says.

The track is based around Chris Maitland's drums: superbly recorded and played. Steven told *Aural Innovations* about the major difference between Chris' playing live and in the studio:

> When you go to see the band live, people do their own thing. Chris is a very, very, very busy drummer. He's like Keith Moon. He doesn't like to settle into grooves. I find it really exciting to play with him on stage, but I don't particularly like that style in the studio. I prefer a more controlled (style) ... which he can do too. He can do anything. But live, he just goes mad ... I think he's one of the best drummers in the world ... I rein him in a little bit in the studio.

The album ends as the track disappears into noise – described by Richard Barbieri on the band's website, as the sound of a Hammond organ: 'A rather ropey specimen ... the sound at the end of the album is the Hammond about to finally die!'

Lightbulb Sun (2000)

Personnel:
Steven Wilson: vocals, guitars, piano, Mellotron, hammered dulcimer, samples, banjo, harp, percussion
Richard Barbieri: synthesizers, synthesized percussion, Hammond organ, Fairground, Fender Rhodes, Clavinet, 'Insects'
Colin Edwin: bass, drum machine, saz, guimbri
Chris Maitland: drums, backing vocals
Eli Hibit: backup rhythm guitar
Strings: Stuart Gordon: violin, viola; Nick Parry: cello – Minerva String Quartet
Recorded at Foel Studio, Llanfair Caereinion, Wales; No Man's Land, Hemel Hempstead, England, November 1999 to January 2000; Christchurch Studios, Bristol, January 2000 (Strings)
Producer: Steven Wilson
Arrangements: Porcupine Tree
Cover Photography: John Foxx
Release date: May 2000
Chart placings: Did not chart
Running time: 56:17
Record label: Kscope

Lightbulb Sun is Porcupine Tree's sixth studio album. It was written very quickly – according to the band's website: 'In three months flat, and within only a few months of the release of the previous one' (*Stupid Dream*).

Unlike other Porcupine Tree albums, there's no overall unifying concept, but most of the songs fall into two broad themes. Wilson said on his website: 'There are at least four or five songs on (the) record, which I call the divorce songs; the relationship songs, which are all about various stages of the splitting up (of) a relationship, of dissolving a relationship. These divorce songs include 'How is Your Life Today?', 'Shesmovedon', 'Hatesong', 'Russia on Ice' and 'Feel So Low'.

The other group of songs are 'nostalgic childhood reminiscences': including 'Lightbulb Sun', the first part of 'Last Chance To Evacuate Planet Earth Before It Is Recycled' and 'Where We Would Be'.

On the band's website, Steven said he'd changed his approach to songwriting on this album:

Lyrically I arrived at a point where I was no longer interested in writing about abstract concepts, like war, religion, space ... etc. ... These are very personal and emotionally raw songs. It took me a long time to have the confidence and experience to be able to write them, and some of them are dripping with negative emotions.

The production is deliberately slightly less-polished than the previous album; consciously moving away from what Steven called the 'stadium sheen' of

Stupid Dream. That doesn't mean the *Lightbulb Sun* production is in any way inferior, but it is noticeable that some of the vocals are much rawer than on other Porcupine Tree albums.

The album certainly features some of the most personal lyrics Steven ever wrote for the band. He told Chris Dick of *Eclipse Magazine* in February 2001, that one of the things that disappointed him about heavy metal was that as much as he loved the heavy riffs, the lyrics were often 'versed in cliché'. Steven was also moving away from the psychedelic tropes of earlier Porcupine Tree albums. He felt that in doing so, he might alienate some of the fans who still wanted him to write about 'nuclear war or science fiction', but he's always tried to move forward with each album and has never worried about losing fans. Generally, he's gained more than he's lost while still resolutely following his own convictions. He said that rather than being inspired by the heavy metal lyrics, his main influence was Pink Floyd's Roger Waters, who 'wrote very personal, very direct lyrics'. This is certainly true of Waters' last Pink Floyd album as a member – *The Final Cut* (1983) – which was based partly on his relationship with his father, who died in battle in Italy during World War II, when Waters was only five months old.

So, were Steven's lyrics on *Lightbulb Sun* written entirely from personal experience? He told Mark Bredius in *Rock Society Magazine* in June 2000 that in writing an album such as this, 'you are also creating something, and can, and do, borrow from art, novels, films and the experiences of friends and family. All of those go into a melting pot, to make something that sounds as though it was written purely from my experience'.

Much later, when talking about 'Bonnie the Cat' – from the final Porcupine Tree album – *The Incident* (2009) – Steven said that the person he'd broken up with had ruined his life. This may well be the same person described in the album's 'divorce' songs. But in a way, it's not important; Steven's personal life should remain personal to him. What *is* important, is the emotional truth of these songs, and also of the songs about childhood. And they do all ring true.

The album's cover art was designed by John Foxx: a member of Ultravox from 1976 to 1979, when he was replaced by Midge Ure. Foxx went on to have a five-year solo career before working as a graphic designer: creating beautiful, vividly-coloured book covers (under his real name, Dennis Leigh) for the first edition of Salman Rushdie's *The Moor's Last Sigh* (1995) and a number of the *Arden Shakespeare* editions.

All music and lyrics by Steven Wilson, except where marked.

'Lightbulb Sun' (5:31)

The title track is a lovely nostalgic song about childhood illness, a topic that could've been given grim treatment on a darker album like those that followed. Here though, the song is mainly a celebration of the strange joy of being at home, enjoying being off school, and lying in bed, tended to by a loving mother: 'And I can watch TV/While I'm wrapped up in bed/And mother makes sure that/I'm watered and fed'.

It feels like a genuine childhood recollection, even including the charming memory of only taking medicine if 'it's followed by sweets', to take away the taste. The idea of the boy in bed, with his curtains closed against the world – 'on my little retreat' – contrasts with that of the boy in the title track of *Fear of a Blank Planet* (2007): trapped behind the bedroom blinds while his teenage hormones rage against his empty world. The two boys have a different view of sunlight as well: in 'Lightbulb Sun', his lightbulb is a 'sun' and a candle is 'a treat'; whereas the boy in 'Fear of a Blank Planet' closes his blinds so tightly, that the real sun cannot get through any gaps.

But 'Lightbulb Sun' is open to much darker interpretations. There's a hint of unease in the slightly sinister image of the boy stuck in his 'bubble of germified air'. The image could be literal, but there's a sense of him being kept in isolation against his will. The idea of smoke filling him as he sleeps could also be disquieting, even though, on the surface, it refers to standard medical treatment.

Some listeners have found an interpretation which is even darker still. This is unlikely to cause Steven a problem, though – as he said in a *Space Rocks Live Forum* on YouTube in November 2020: 'I think that's something fundamental to music, that everyone has their own interpretation. Many people have come to me with interpretations of my songs that are nothing like what I intended, but that doesn't mean they are any less valid. I love that about the fact that lyrics are infinitely interpretable, in that sense'.

The song begins with acoustic guitars that appear to burst in halfway through a chord sequence, giving a sense of urgency as if we're glimpsing a half-formed thought; a joyful entry into nostalgia for childhood, emphasised through almost childlike vocal purity. Slide guitar parts (similar to those on 'Even Less' on *Stupid Dream*) lead to a more aggressive section; the shouted backing vocals giving an almost punk feel: 'My head beats a better way/Tomorrow's a better day'.

Also remarkable is the simple vocal line: repeated many times but without feeling repetitive. This is a tribute to not only Steven Wilson's skill as a writer who constantly defies conventional song structures but to the band's rich variety of instrumental skills. In particular, Colin Edwin's bass part propels the music, and Chris Maitland's explosive drum fill at one point threatens to derail the song, but adds to the drama. Steven's guitar-playing is also excellent, particularly the solo.

The song ends with the sound of children playing in the street, reminding the boy of the friends he's missing while he's ill in bed. Similar sounds end another song about school children: Pink Floyd's 'Another Brick In The Wall (Part 2)' from *The Wall* (1979): although those children seem to be enjoying their play, the taunts of the manic school teacher, threaten, as he shouts, 'If you don't eat your meat, you can't have any pudding!'. It seems Roger Waters had a much less happy childhood than Steven Wilson.

'How Is Your Life Today?' (2:46)

This is the first of the album's songs which Steven described as a 'divorce' song. It's a melancholy waltz, driven by simple piano chords but with no drums, which is unusual for a Porcupine Tree track. In its elegant simplicity and brevity, it's like a song by Blackfield: Steven's collaboration with Israeli rock musician and singer Aviv Geffen. The two started collaborating in 2000, when Geffen invited Porcupine Tree to tour Israel; though their debut album – *Blackfield* – wasn't released until 2004 (2005 in the US). The band's been an outlet for Steven's more straightforward pop songs.

This track also has gorgeous vocal harmonies. Steven told Pete Pardo of *Sea of Tranquility* in November 2001: 'My interest musically has shifted from abstract instrumental music to a more concise and crafted songwriting and vocal arrangement. Everything really changed for me a few years ago, when I went through my born-again Brian Wilson (of The Beach Boys) is God conversion!'

Lyrically, the song marks the early stages of a breakup, the narrator's former partner having left. This leaves him depressed, allowing the post to 'pile up in the hallway' – perhaps addressed to her. The chorus is a bittersweet inquiry about what her life is like now that she's left him; perhaps showing genuine interest in what she's doing now, but more likely bitterly reflecting on the fact that he's no longer in touch with her and has no way of finding out how she's really getting on. The most evocative lines relate to the moment she left: 'I was kissed on the cheek by a cold mouth/While the taxi was waiting like a getaway car'. The coldness of her mouth is metaphorical as well as literal, and she kisses him on the cheek rather than on the lips, marking the distance between them. The taxi – 'like a getaway car' – reflects her desperation to get away as quickly as possible. (The cold lips and getaway car have caused some online commentators to suspect that foul play, possibly murder or suicide, is involved). The scene is rounded off by the cat staring at the narrator as all this happens: probably in that sardonic way that cats do.

Keyboard player, Richard Barbieri, is credited with playing 'Fairground': a synthesized fairground organ, of the type accompanying riders as they circle gently up and down on mechanical merry-go-round horses. Richard and Steven designed the sound specifically for this track. The Beatles' producer, George Martin, carried out a similar fairground sound recreation (but more painstaking due to the limited technology at the time). According to Ian MacDonald in *Revolution in the Head* (Revised Edition, Pimlico 1995), John Lennon asked Martin to make a fairground sound assimilation so realistic, that 'you could smell the sawdust': for the song 'Being for the Benefit of Mr. Kite!' from *Sgt. Pepper's Lonely Hearts Club Band* (1967). It's unlikely that Steven was unaware of Martin's fairground sound since Steven grew up listening to *Sgt. Pepper*. Wilson's sound perhaps suggests childhood nostalgia, but it also seems to be part of his intention to widen the album's instrumental palette.

'Four Chords That Made a Million' (3:36)

This was one of only two Porcupine Tree singles that ever charted in the UK. It reached number 84 in May 2000. (The other was 'Shesmovedon'). It was released to promote the forthcoming album, but in the context of that album, it's a strange anomaly. On his website, Steven Wilson says the song 'doesn't have any relation to anything else on the album, or anything else I've ever written'. The theme is a fairly familiar one, the crassness with which the recording industry treats music and musicians, and perhaps again reflects Steven's continuing disappointment with his relative lack of commercial success. The fact that a song can be successful – making 'a million' – despite only using four chords (presumably a simple chord sequence, as used in many pop songs) is frustrating to an endlessly inventive songwriter. The English band, Status Quo, were famously called 'Three Chord Quo' because they allegedly used only three chords in their songs; the band themselves joyfully embraced that idea, by titling their 2007 album, *In Search of the Fourth Chord*. (At the time of writing, they've had nearly 60 top 40 singles in the UK).

It's unclear whether this song is a clever 1960s pastiche or a punk protest song: it ends up failing as either. It begins promisingly enough, with a catchy distorted guitar riff, and percussion that could've come from Indian music, sounding rather like some of The Beatles' experiments. But the distorted, almost punk-sounding vocals sound odd coming from Wilson. The lyrics lack his usual subtlety and poetry; calling a record company executive 'a moron with a cheque book', doesn't equal the biting satire of 'Come in here, dear boy, have a cigar': Roy Harper's delivery, piercingly cynical on Pink Floyd's 'Have a Cigar' (*Wish You Were Here*, (1975).

During a Twitter Listening Party hosted by The Charlatans' Tim Burgess in July 2020, Steven said 'The Sound of Muzak' (from the next album *In Absentia*) was a more satisfying track about the music industry: 'I had previously touched on the theme with 'Four Chords That Made a Million' ... but that track didn't really work musically or lyrically. This time around, I got it right, I think.'

'Four Chords That Made A Million' does, however feature a short, slightly-redeeming section, where Steven goes into a seemingly heartfelt reverie about how he's tried and died – 'trying to get through' – with a chord sequence (consisting of more than four chords in just a few bars) worthy of a James Bond movie theme. But the punky chorus' brutal return breaks the spell.

'Shesmovedon' (5:13)

The album's second single reached number 85 (in July 2000) and number 4 in the *NME* (*New Musical Express*) independent singles chart.

It's another 'divorce' song, marking a relationship's acrimonious end. The bitter sentiment is emphasised through the casual, offhand delivery of the title as a single composite word: 'shesmovedon': suggesting how carelessly the narrator's former lover cast him off, leaving him to wonder, 'Did we connect? Or was it all just biding time for you?'

A casual listen could suggest that this is a love song, as the glorious, warm and mellow chorus harmonies seem at odds with the bitter lyric. The lyric's cynicism is revealed around two and a half minutes in, when the words 'she's moved on' are half-whispered intimately into one ear, then the other: a subtle way of expressing the narrator's suffering.

The song begins with a powerful guitar riff and ends with an excellent guitar solo that screams almost with pain, before breaking up completely. There is something very satisfying about the verse chord sequence, and the rougher side of Steven's voice is used to great effect in the chorus vocal harmonies.

'Last Chance To Evacuate Planet Earth Before It Is Recycled' (4:48)

This crashes straight in from the previous song, with the jangling sound of a banjo; Steven's vocal delivery almost like a folk singer. We're in his childhood nostalgia world. As he said on the band's site:

> There is a whole set of songs (on this album) where the pastoral sound of long-gone English summers, exerts its influence on me (not for the first time). In a song like 'Winding Shot', there are shades of Crosby, Stills, Nash &Young, and Nick Drake, although the end result is, hopefully, pure Porcupine Tree.

Steven has always had the ability to create these evocative childhood images. Much later, in 'Ancestral' (from *Hand. Cannot. Erase* in 2015), he uses few words to evoke a powerfully nostalgic image: 'A bicycle/A garden wall/A mother's call' – rekindling memories of long hot summer holidays, 'climbing a tree or two'.

The first part of the song is called 'A Winding Shot (Summer 1981)', and refers to the time when childhood turns to adolescence. In the summer of 1981, Steven was thirteen and living in Hemel Hempstead: an English town located about 24 miles northwest of London. Winding Shot is the name of a small cul-de-sac off Spring Lane in Hemel Hempstead.

Steven returned to his Hemel Hempstead childhood, on 'Perfect Life', from his solo album, *Hand. Cannot. Erase*. The spoken introduction (delivered by the female protagonist) includes these words:

> When I was thirteen, I had a sister for six months. Sometimes we would head down to Blackbirds Moor to watch the barges on Grand Union in the twilight.

Steven told *FaceCulture* in a YouTube interview in January 2015, that Blackbirds Moor is a park near his childhood home and that the Grand Union canal runs through the town:

> And I absolutely remember as a child, going down to the park on a beautiful summer evening, with my friend, and watching the barges go past on the

canal. So that is a very vivid but real image from my childhood, and I gave it to my character.

It's interesting to note that the character in each song is thirteen. The nostalgia in this song is tinged with regret as summer comes to an end: 'Summer went away/And we just weren't the same.' This part of the song ends with his childhood friend kissing him on the lips, as they reach that strange limbo of adolescence: suspended between childhood and adulthood; 'Not grown-ups but not kids'.

A rhythmic acoustic riff drives a short bridge, leading to an instrumental passage from which the song title is derived. The title could be an environmental message: something that's become even more important in the two decades since the song was written. But Steven told Joakim Jahlmar of *DPRP.net* in March 2001: 'Last Chance To Evacuate Planet Earth Before It Is Recycled' is not about ecology. It takes its title from the edited transcript of a videotape dated 29 September 1996, from the leader of the Heaven's Gate religious cult, who called himself Do (real name: Marshall Applewhite).

This planet is about to be recycled, refurbished, started over. That doesn't mean it's going to be destroyed; it doesn't mean it's the end of the world. And whether or not you believe that this civilization is going to be recycled or refurbished is up to you. Now, the purpose of this tape is to warn you that this is about to happen and that it's going to happen very soon. At the End of the Age, the planet is wiped clean... refurbished... rejuvenated.

On 22 March 1997, Heaven's Gate published a macabre press release:

'HEAVEN'S GATE 'Away Team' Returns to Level Above Human in Distant Space' By the time you receive this, we'll be gone – several dozen of us. We came from the Level Above Human in distant space, and we have now exited the bodies that we were wearing for our earthly task, to return to the world from whence we came – task completed.

Applewhite told his followers that they could leave Earth on a spaceship that accompanied the comet, Hale-Bopp, that was due to approach the planet in early 1997. Tragically – despite a claim on the Heaven's Gate website that the group was strongly against suicide – 39 cult members (including Applewhite) were found dead in a San Diego house on 26 March 1997.

The track ends with the song title's chilling words, spoken by Applewhite before he joined his followers in a mass suicide, achieved by consuming a mixture of apple sauce, vodka and barbiturates.

The gentle music of the song's first part blossoms into a more complex instrumental, with more urgent drumming and a busier bass line. The gradual morphing from nostalgia into disturbing rhetoric about Earth's future is an unexpected transition. It reflects another aspect of Steven Wilson's interest in humanity's darker side, as he explained to Joakim Jahlmar:

> Religion is always one of those things which has fascinated me in a kind of negative way, if you like. It is something which has fascinated me in a kind of gruesome way ... it's not people who have spiritual beliefs, but it's the politics of religion and the commercial side of religion – which, in some ways, is the sickest and most disturbing form of politics we have on this Earth, because it masquerades as something else.

Steven returned to the theme of religious cults in 'The Blind House' on *The Incident* (2009), which referred to Warren Jeffs' cult at the Yearning for Zion Ranch in Texas.

'The Rest Will Flow' (3:24)

This is a straightforward pop song, and indeed the original plan was for it to be released as a single. According to the band's website at the time: 'A planned October release for a third single from the album – 'The Rest Will Flow' – has been cancelled, but the single may now be issued to coincide with a major headlining tour in early 2001.' For some unexplained reason, the single didn't materialise, which is a pity, as it's a very attractive song. There's a lovely Dave Gregory string arrangement, with performers from the Minerva String Quartet, whose website describes them working with 'cult pop group, Porcupine Tree'. Though it wouldn't always be accurate to describe the band as a 'pop group', in this case, the description seems reasonable.

The song acts as a brief respite between the dystopian world of the previous song, and the vitriol of the next. It describes a moment of hope in the narrator's life: 'Then out of darkness I found I could still feel/Something good/ Stay with me my angel/I found you/Now I don't feel so low.'

It would be good to be able to say this track shows Wilson turning a corner after the bitter breakup described elsewhere on the album, but there's no suggestion that this is the case. It's probably better just to take it at face value as a simple, charming love song.

'Hatesong' (Edwin, Wilson) (8:26)

After the previous track's moment of calm, this 'divorce song' drips with vitriol. This is not a love song: as Public Image Ltd sang in their 1983 top five UK hit titled with that phrase. That song was about commerce – 'Big business is very wise/I'm inside free enterprise' – whereas 'Hatesong' is about hatred. When playing it live, Wilson sometimes introduced it as 'an antidote' to all the love songs sung by boy bands and girl bands; but that perhaps distracts from the fact that this is an intensely personal song about the end of a relationship.

Steven's verse vocals are disingenuously sweet; almost innocent, reminding us that hatred – like revenge – is sometimes a dish best served cold. There's a

Above: Steven Wilson, founder, principal songwriter, lead vocalist, guitarist and sometime keyboard player for Porcupine Tree. (*Alamy*)

Left: Cassettes released by the earliest version of Porcupine Tree, which features the young Steven Wilson pretending to be a band. (*Delerium*)

Right: A version of the band from around 1995, which includes percussionist Rick Edwards, who played percussion on 'Moonloop' on *The Sky Moves Sideways*.

Left: The first complete line-up. Clockwise from left: Colin Edwin (bass), Chris Maitland (drums), Steven Wilson (vocals and guitar), Richard Barbieri (keyboards).

Right: *On The Sunday Of Life*, the first studio album by Porcupine Tree on Delerium Records. A woman dives into a rural landscape. (*Kscope, Delerium*)

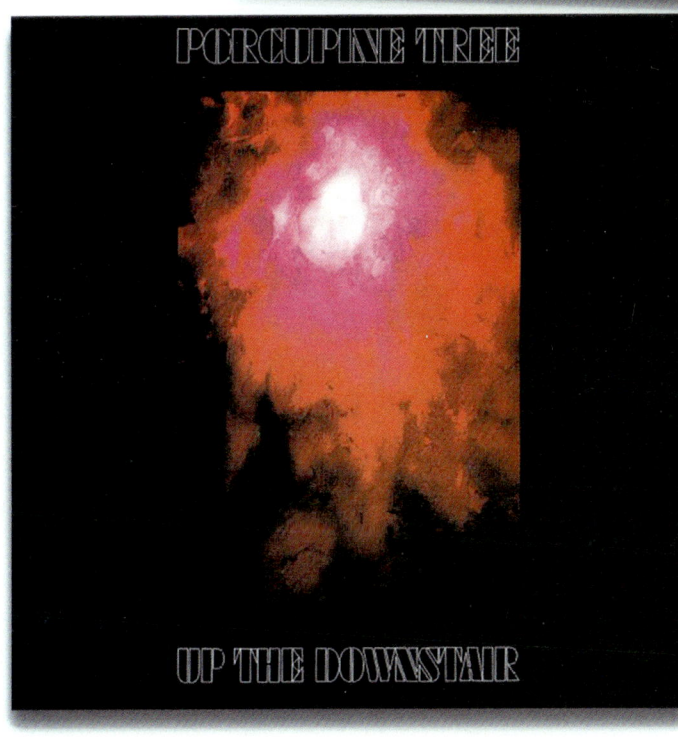

Left: Although joined occasionally by Colin Edwin and Richard Barbieri, the second studio album *Up The Downstair* was still largely a solo Steven Wilson project. (*Delerium*)

Left: For the band's third album, *The Sky Moves Sideways,* Steven Wilson was joined for the first time by drummer Chris Maitland. (*Delerium*)

Right: Steven Wilson saw this photo and immediately thought it would make a good front cover for *Signify*, the band's fourth studio album. (*Kscope*)

Right and below: Images from the artwork for Porcupine Tree's fifth studio album, *Stupid Dream*, showing music as a product produced in a sterile factory environment. (*Kscope*)

porcupine tree stupid dream

Left: The cover of Porcupine Tree's sixth studio album *Lightbulb Sun.* The title track describes a boy off sick from school. (*Kscope*)

Right: *Recordings,* a compilation of B-sides and unreleased tracks from the *Stupid Dream* and *Lightbulb Sun* era. (*Kscope*)

Right and below: The band's seventh and eighth studio albums, *In Absentia* and *Deadwing* were the first to feature artwork by Lasse Hoile. Gavin Harrison replaced Chris Maitland as the band's drummer. (*Kscope/Lava*)

This page: Images from Porcupine Tree's first live DVD, *Arriving Somewhere...* From the top: Steven Wilson, Colin Edwin and John Wesley, who toured with the band during this period providing second guitar and backing vocals. (*Kscope*)

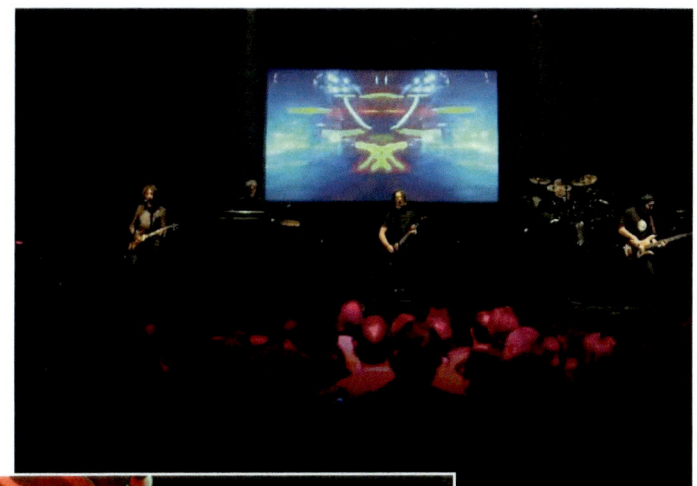

This page: Images from the *Anesthetize* live DVD. From the top; the whole band, Gavin Harrison, with his impressive drum kit and keyboard player Richard Barbieri. (*Kscope*)

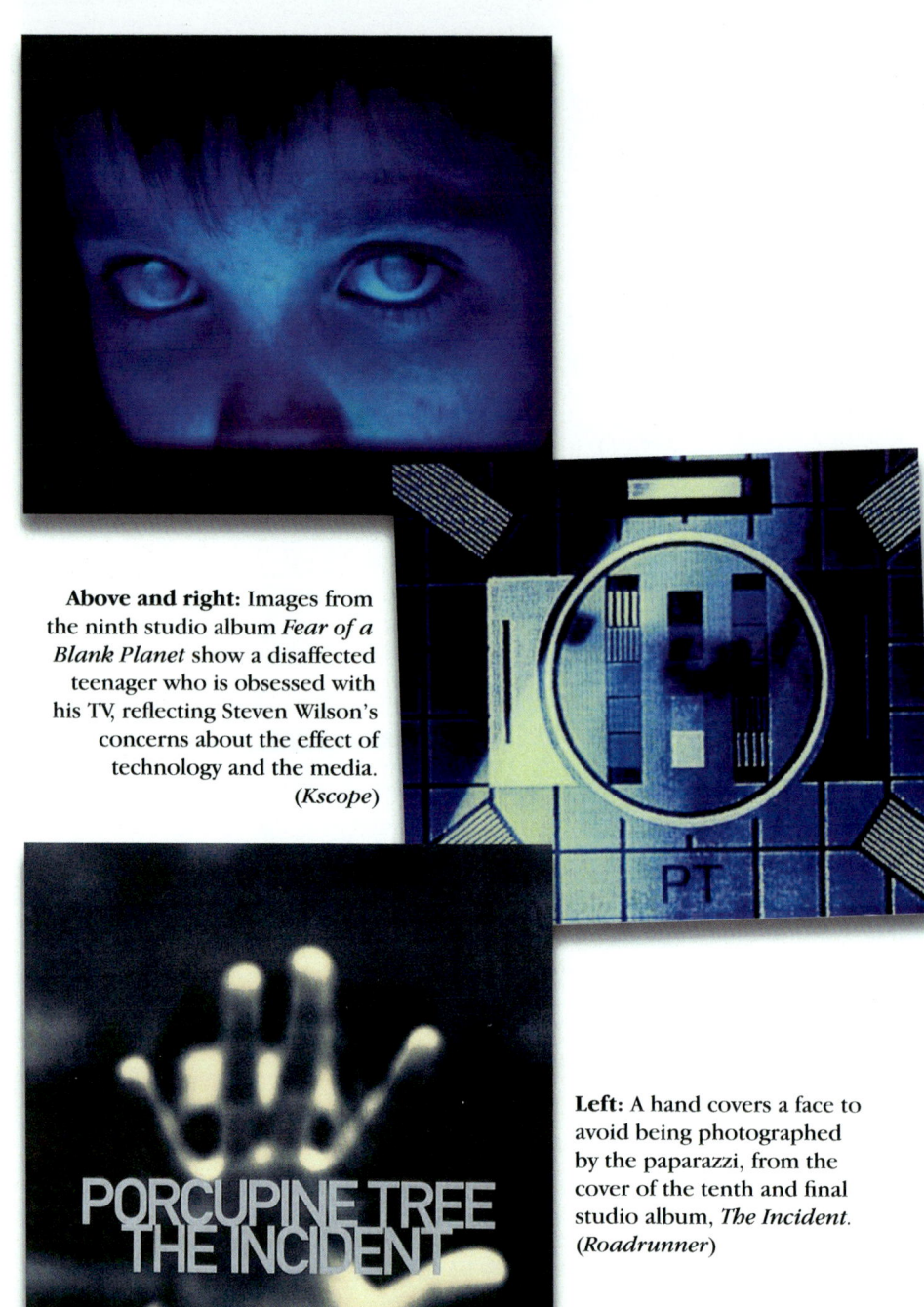

Above and right: Images from the ninth studio album *Fear of a Blank Planet* show a disaffected teenager who is obsessed with his TV, reflecting Steven Wilson's concerns about the effect of technology and the media. (*Kscope*)

Left: A hand covers a face to avoid being photographed by the paparazzi, from the cover of the tenth and final studio album, *The Incident*. (*Roadrunner*)

This page: Covers for three singles: 'Waiting' (from *Signify*), 'Piano Lessons' (from *Stupid Dream*) and '4 Chords That Made a Million' (from *Lightbulb Sun*). (*Delerium*, *Kscope*)

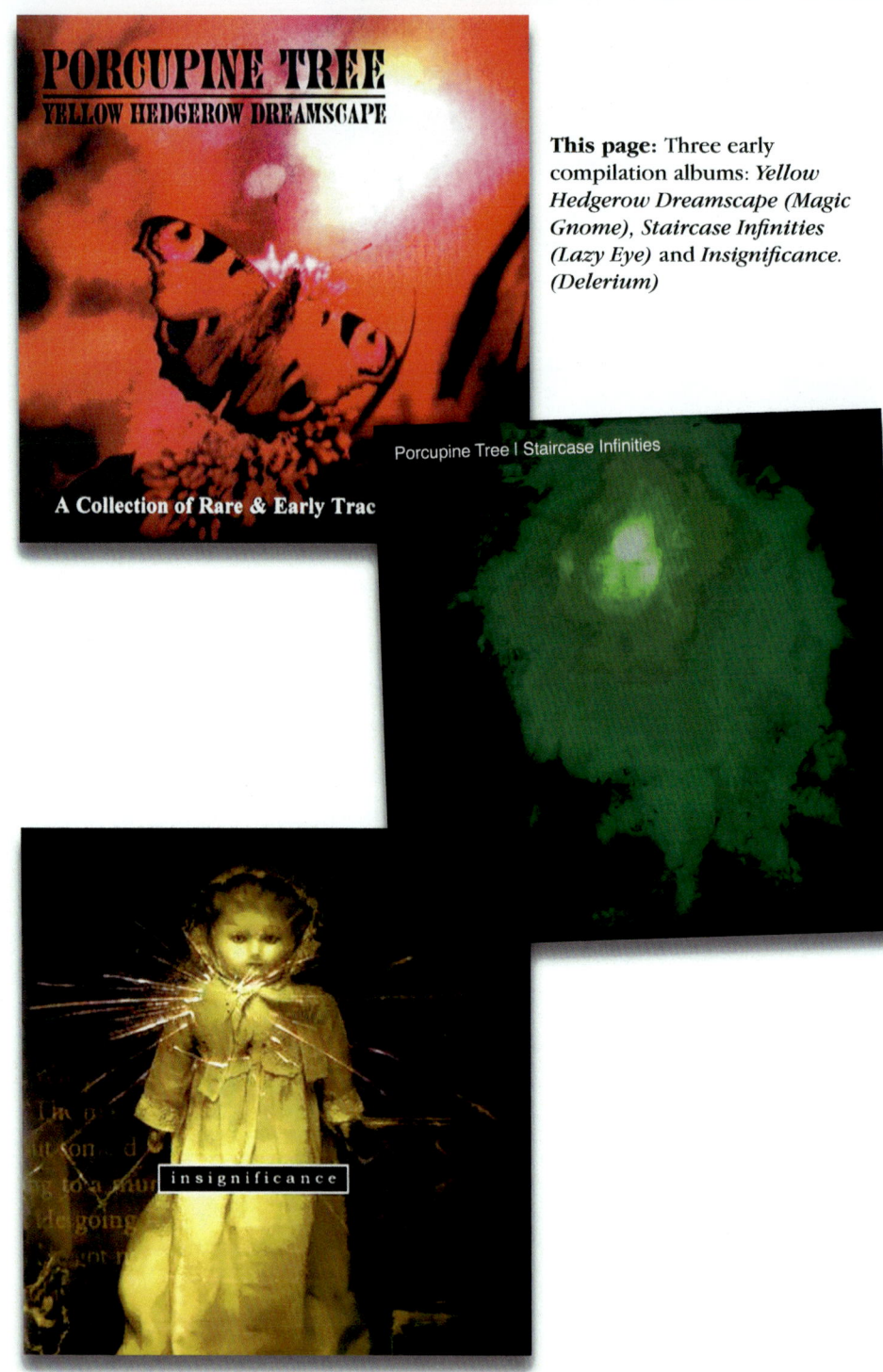

PORCUPINE TREE
YELLOW HEDGEROW DREAMSCAPE

A Collection of Rare & Early Trac

Porcupine Tree I Staircase Infinities

insignificance

This page: Three early compilation albums: *Yellow Hedgerow Dreamscape (Magic Gnome), Staircase Infinities (Lazy Eye)* and *Insignificance. (Delerium)*

Porcupine Tree | Metanoia

Right: *Metanoia* a collection of instrumental improvisations, recorded during the *Signify* sessions. (*Delerium*)

PORCUPINE TREE

VOYAGE 34
THE COMPLETE TRIP

Left and below: Different versions of the cover of the *Voyage 34* compilation. (*Delerium, Kscope*)

Porcupine Tree | Voyage 34

Porcupine Tree | Stars Die | The Delerium Years 1991 - 1997

Left: The cover of the double album compilation *Stars Die: The Delerium Years 1991–1997,* released by Kscope in 2002. *(Kscope)*

porcupine tree / nil recurring

Right: The cover of the *Nil Recurring* EP, a spin-off from *Fear of a Blank Planet* sharing that album's theme of disaffected youth. *(Kscope)*

Left: The cover of the thirteen-CD box set *Porcupine Tree: The Delerium Years 1991-1997* released by Transmission Recordings in 2020. *(Transmission)*

This page: Covers of three live albums: *Coma Divine* (*Delerium*), *Arriving Somewhere…* (*Kscope/Snapper/Burning Shed*), and *Octane Twisted.* (*Kscope*)

Porcupine Tree | Coma Divine
Recorded Live in Rome

Porcupine Tree /// Arriving somewhere...

PORCUPINE TREE
OCTANE TWISTED

This page: Posters for tours early and late in the band's career, over two decades apart. The band first played live in 1993 and last played together in 2010. (*Transmission*)

fascinating contrast with the song 'Betrayed' by Peter Hammill (lead singer and songwriter of progressive rock band, Van der Graaf Generator), from his 1977 solo album *Over*: one of the rawest and most visceral break-up albums ever made. He virtually screams his view on hate: 'It seems that there is nothing left but hatred and lust in the world.' Each writer shares the sentiment that he has suffered more, as a result of the break-up: 'I'm more cut up than you.' Steven also invites the addressee to respond to his hatred: 'I hope when you hear this, you'll want to sue.'

Steven co-wrote the song with bass player Colin Edwin, and the bass part is an album highlight, particularly in the introduction, where he combines a funky style with subtle harmonics. Keyboard player Richard Barbieri cleverly picks up on the harmonics, adding an icy synth wash. As is often the case with funk, the space between the notes is as important as the notes themselves: a mantra followed by Miles Davis, amongst many others. It feels as if there are nearly two beats of silence between each of the bass riff repeats. There's an even more effective use of space from around 3:30, when the bass line creates a sense of anticipation and release each time. Colin told Scott Kahn of *MusicPlayers.com* in December 2010 that he'd picked up some unusual instruments on his travels: 'I'd been to Turkey, and I picked up a thing called a saz, which is a sort of Turkish lute with a very long neck ... and that ended up being on 'Hatesong', which has been a live favourite for years'. The instrument he's referring to is a Bas ba lama (bass saz): a long-necked Turkish lute with built-in electronics and bass-guitar machine heads (the tuning mechanism at the top of the neck). In the song's live versions, Colin usually played a Wal bass: a name that's become revered amongst bass players.

Colin's bass-playing is matched by Steven's powerful guitar solos, channelling the American nu-metal band, Korn, as he said on the Porcupine Tree site: 'One of the solos of 'Hatesong', I call my *Korn solo*, on account of the fact that the bottom strings on the guitar are tuned down so low that the notes can be bent several tones. Four minutes in – a lot of string bending! Another solo (circa) seven minutes in, much higher up the fretboard!'

At around seven minutes in, drummer, Chris Maitland, gets the chance to shine, providing a sparse rhythm, syncopated against Colin's bass line; while Steven's bluesy echo-drenched guitar riffs float high above. The track has a real feeling of being a band effort, showing off all their virtuosic talents and improvisatory skills, and it's easy to see why they enjoyed playing it live.

'Where We Would Be' (4:12)

This is another of the album's nostalgia songs, giving a break from the divorce songs on either side of it. The premise is simple: two children looking forward to the future, and imagining where they would be in their lives: 'Strange how you never become/The person you see when you're young'. Steven as a child, imagines himself writing songs while his future partner paints: giving her creative agency in a way which Peter Hammill denies his partner in another song from his 1977 album *Over* – 'On Tuesdays She Used To Do Yoga' – where he slumps in front of the TV, 'Always ready to say to myself/That I was an artist/ Implying that she was not'.

As in other nostalgic songs, 'Where We Would Be' describes a time when 'We knew that the sun would shine': the perpetual summer of childhood memories. Various online commentators have suggested that the song could be about two young friends or lovers who had an acrimonious split later on or even that she died. But these interpretations would place the song more in the 'divorce' category than the 'nostalgia' category. It seems unlikely that Steven would be nostalgic about earlier times in a relationship that ended in a bitter split. It's more likely that the two of them just grew apart naturally or lost touch. What these commentators have picked up on is the wistful sense of sadness permeating the song, onto which listeners can project their own sorrow and regret.

The vocal delivery is deliberately unpolished – and unprocessed compared with many of Steven's other productions – creating a more personal and direct style matching his wish to communicate more directly about his life.

On the band's website, Steven described the guitar solo as the best he'd written to date: influenced by the sound of American industrial rock band, Nine Inch Nails' 1999 double album *The Fragile*: 'There was also an influence from industrial and metal music coming through ... part of the beauty of the guitar solo, comes from the fact that it was played relatively straight, but then fed through so many distortion and lo-fi processes, that it began to fizz and disintegrate.'

'Russia on Ice' (Part I (Wilson); Part II Instrumental (Barbieri, Edwin, Maitland, Wilson)) (13:03)

This song is divided into two parts, the second of which is an instrumental written by the whole band.

Part I

Part one is another divorce song, with a melancholy, brooding atmosphere. 'Hatesong''s bitter invective has turned to deep depression, reflected in the very different bass line made up of only two notes (E and F#) – not the sophisticated funk of 'Hatesong'. But this doesn't make it a lesser song; it succeeds in creating its own bleak soundscape, which matches the emotional landscape it describes.

The vocal melody is as simple as the bass line; based around a minor third – the first and third notes of the scale of E minor. For most listeners brought up in the western music tradition, the minor key represents sadness, and the constant return to the minor third stresses the mournful nature. Steven's vocal delivery is suitably resigned, only becoming a little more animated in the chorus.

The lyrics are rather obscure and introspective, although the opening lines are very direct: 'You think I deserve this/You said I was stupid'. His thoughts are 'like coal', presumably reflecting their blackness. The words 'Russia on Ice' could refer to vodka and relate to the drinking problem referred to later in the song. The phrase could also refer to the narrator's emotional landscape: an icy Siberian winter.

The first guitar solo suddenly stops, as if giving up: rather like the narrator. The second solo sounds rather like Mikael Åkerfeldt of Swedish band Opeth.

Part I builds to an emotional climax, with cinematic strings and widescreen backing vocals, suggesting a slight thawing of the icy atmosphere; but, 'Nothing melts in this cold' – any release from pain, is suspended, while the pain itself continues to 'burn a hole'.

Part II

Part II is an opportunity for the whole band to show off their instrumental skills. This section begins with a bass solo from Colin Edwin. He told Scott Kahn: 'I'd been to North Africa for a while, and I had this thing called a guimbri, which is a three-string bass instrument ... There's a thing that sounds like a rubber band, and that's me playing the guimbri.'

The languid pace so far suddenly picks up, as morose introspection turns to anger. Part I's dominating minor third interval is now replaced with the tritone (augmented 4th) – or 'the devil in music' – as ambient music suddenly turns into heavy metal. This is a brief vision of the much heavier sound the band would embrace for the next four albums (beginning with *In Absentia* in 2002). Pounding kick-drum beats – which could've come straight from a dance or disco song – lead to a funky break-out section, with a guitar wah-wah effect adding to the dance feel, before the heavy metal riff returns. Despite the subject matter, you can feel the band enjoying themselves. A section of industrial funk follows: this could almost be King Crimson from their 1995 album, *THRAK* – even down to Chris Maitland's explosively rhythmic drums. All the while, Richard Barbieri's subtle keyboard washes add to the sense of alienation. Never one to do showy solos of the kind beloved of many prog-rock keyboard players, Barbieri merely heightens the emotional depth – in many Porcupine Tree songs.

On the band's site, Steven said he and Richard 'worked on creating some unique keyboard sounds for the album – e.g. the insects at the end of 'Russia on Ice''.

'Feel So Low' (5:18)

The album's last track is another divorce song: an uncomplicated ballad with a simple message, clearly expressed in the title. It seems to relate specifically to Steven's life; even referring to his attempts to contact his former lover at Christmas in 1998. On the band's site, he said that the song 'pleased me a lot, as I resisted the temptation to refine the original stream-of-consciousness words, and left the nerve-ends dangling'.

The vocal is almost spoken, rather than sung, the opening words delivered on one note. It feels like a song that's been improvised, without the complex crafting that goes into most of Steven's work: perfectly expressing the sense of resignation he feels at the end of the relationship. It's more like a song from a solo album – there's no bass line, drums or percussion. But there are some keyboard parts, on (what sounds like) a Mellotron, and a lovely string arrangement.

Blackfield also recorded the song, releasing it as a bonus on various versions of their first album, *Blackfield* (2004). Live versions of the song included an extended instrumental section at the end.

In Absentia (2002)

Personnel:
Steven Wilson: vocals, acoustic and electric guitar, piano, keyboards, banjo
Richard Barbieri: analogue synths, Mellotron, Hammond organ, keyboards
Colin Edwin: bass
Gavin Harrison: drums, percussion
Aviv Geffen: backing vocals
John Wesley: backing vocals, guitar
Recorded at Avatar Studios, New York, USA; Air Lyndhurst, London, UK; No Man's
Land, Hemel Hempstead, UK; New Rising, Colchester, UK; Red Room Recorders,
Tampa, Florida, USA
Producer: Steven Wilson
Mixer: Tim Palmer
Release dates: Original edition: September 2002; Deluxe Edition: February 2020
Chart placings: Did not chart
Running time: 40:24
Record label: Lava (Atlantic)
Current release: Kscope

In Absentia is Porcupine Tree's seventh studio album. It marks several major changes for the band. Gavin Harrison replaced Chris Maitland on drums. The musical style moved from the psychedelia, space rock, trance, prog rock and art rock of previous albums, to a new hybrid: progressive metal, maintaining the melodic strength and rich vocal harmonies. The band also moved from indie record label, Snapper, to Lava Records: part of Atlantic Records in America.

They recorded large parts of the album in New York at the Power Station (at the time known as Avatar Studios). It was also the first album for which Danish artist, Lasse Hoile, provided the visuals. Hoile created a very strong visual language: for live shows, videos and album covers for the rest of Porcupine Tree's career.

In Steven's view – expressed in a Twitter Listening Party with Tim Burgess (lead singer of The Charlatans) in July 2020 – *In Absentia* was 'our best album', but he also saw it as '...the beginning of the end ... It did become harder to redefine the band's sound after *In Absentia*. After three more albums using this musical vocabulary, I felt it was time to end the band on a high and do different things.'

In Absentia is a Latin phrase that can refer, in criminal legal cases, to someone being tried in their absence: not physically present in court. It can also refer to receiving an academic award or being excommunicated from the church without being there. In the context of the album, perhaps a darker meaner is more appropriate: it can also refer to the legal declaration of someone's death, despite the fact that no body or human remains have been found. On his website, Steven Wilson gives this explanation:

It's related to some of the lyrics. It's about people on the fringes, on the edges of humanity and society. I have an interest in serial killers, child molesters and wife beaters ... not in what they did, but in the psychology of why. What caused them to become unhinged and twisted? Why are they unable to empathise? It's sort of a metaphor – there's something missing, a black hole, a cancer in their soul. It's an absence in the soul.

Steven Wilson has a fascination for the human psyche's dark side: in particular, the minds of serial killers. The theme recurs in 'Raider II' – from his second solo album, *Grace for Drowning* (2011) – which is based on Dennis Rader: the American serial killer known by the acronym BTK (Bind, Torture, Kill). The BTK Strangler killed ten people in Kansas between 1974 and 1991.

The question arises as to the extent to which *In Absentia* is a concept album about a serial killer. This theory is difficult to sustain in relation to tracks like 'The Sound of Muzak' (about the way the music industry is destroying real music) and 'Trains' (more childhood nostalgia). There's no doubt that some of the songs are about serial killers: including 'Blackest Eyes', 'The Creator Has a Mastertape' and 'Strip the Soul'. The track '.3' was originally part of 'Strip the Soul', so may also qualify, and 'Wedding Nails' is an instrumental but may have a peripheral link. Two other tracks relate to the wider theme of an 'absence in the soul': 'Heartattack in a Layby' tells of a lonely and empty death in tragically mundane circumstances, and 'Prodigal' describes a lonely misfit. The important point is that – in Steven Wilson's words – the title is 'related to *some* of the lyrics'.

As Wilson said in the 2020 Twitter Listening Party, the album artwork relates to the theme of 'something being missing ... Lasse's artwork continues it by including photos of people and idyllic settings that have been scratched out by a frenzied knife'. The image eventually chosen for the front cover immediately struck Steven: 'It was the first time I ever worked with this genius. I think he sent some of his work in to my manager, and the moment I saw the image, I said out loud: 'That's the cover!'

The cover is a very disturbing Lasse self-portrait, in which his eye seems to have rolled up inside his head, leaving only the whites showing. The blankness in the eyes, relating to the blankness in the soul, is an important theme of the album. This becomes a recurring theme on later album covers. *Deadwing* shows the back of a woman's head, so the eyes cannot be seen. *Fear of a Blank Planet* has the blank eyes of a teenager. *The Incident* shows a hand covering a face so the eyes can't be seen. Steven's solo albums take up the theme. A gas mask covers his face on the *Insurgentes* cover. On the cover of *The Raven That Refused to Sing*, the ghost's eyes are blank, as are the eyes of the figure on the related album, *Drive Home*. Steven's eyes can barely be seen on the cover of *Cover Version*, and they are closed on *To the Bone*. It's fascinating that the *windows to the soul* are closed, blank or obscured in these images.

In Absentia is the first Porcupine Tree album to feature the band's new drummer, Gavin Harrison, then known mainly for his work as a session musician. More recently, he's made solo albums and also recorded with Canadian bass player, Antoine Fafard. At the time of writing, Gavin is one of King Crimson's three live drummers, and is also a member of The Pineapple Thief.

Porcupine Tree needed a new drummer because Chris Maitland – who'd played on all the previous albums where there was a drummer – left the band. It's remarkable that Porcupine Tree otherwise kept the same line-up throughout its history, considering the number of musicians who have come and gone from bands like Yes. But Chris' departure from Porcupine Tree remains a delicate issue. At the time, the band's website simply said, 'Porcupine Tree's long-term drummer – Chris Maitland – ceased to be a member of the band in February for personal reasons. We would like to wish him well for the future, and thank him for his distinctive and powerful contribution to the band over the past eight years'.

In August 2020, Steven told Dave Everley of *Prog* magazine that Chris was 'becoming increasingly anxious at giving up a lucrative regular job playing West End shows, and this anxiety turned to tension'. Steven said: 'Chris wasn't concentrating properly and wasn't playing as well as he should have done. I lost my temper, and it resulted in a parting of the ways'. As Everley points out, the two were later sufficiently reconciled for Chris to appear on Blackfield's 2004 debut album.

Steven told Anil Prasad of *Innerviews.org* in 2004, that for a long time, he'd been resistant to the idea of signing a major label deal; preferring the individual attention the band could receive as the biggest act on a small label, rather than being 'a small fish in a big pond'. He was approached by Andy Leff: an American music manager who was a Porcupine Tree fan. He, in turn, put Steven in touch with Andy Karp: an A&R executive at Lava Records, New York, who was also a genuine fan of the band. Steven was persuaded by the fact that both were real music fans – unlike many other record company executives of the time. He told Dave Everley: 'I got very excited about the possibilities of making a record for a major American label, with all the attendant promotion and financial input that would imply.'

Lava did provide substantial financial resources, amounting to around $400,000, including tour support. But sadly, the new relationship didn't bring the success that both sides had anticipated. Steven told Anil Prasad that *In Absentia* had sold about three times as many as previous albums worldwide: a total of around 100,000 at that time. In particular, it had done far better in North America: 'We've gone literally from selling 2,000 copies to 45,000 copies'. It's difficult to estimate what the album sales have been since. It seems likely that *In Absentia* has continued to sell in reasonable numbers, partly because fans of Porcupine Tree's style of music may prefer CD or vinyl to streaming. But the streaming figures are healthy too: as of July 2021, the album's three most popular songs – 'Trains', 'Blackest Eyes' and 'The Sound of Muzak' – had collectively received around 45,000,000 Spotify plays; and another fan favourite – 'Lazarus' from *Deadwing* – had been played 13,500,000 times, making a total of nearly 60,000,000 plays for these four songs.

So why was the album, in relative terms, a commercial failure at the time? Diplomatic and fair-minded as ever, Steven has not been in a hurry to simply blame Lava. He appreciated that Porcupine Tree was in some ways a hard sell – not due to the lack of quality or appeal of the music, but because of the band's eclecticism, as he told Anil Prasad: 'How do you market a band that one minute is playing metal, the next minute is playing trip hop, and the next minute is playing progressive rock?' He also described the band as 'this bunch of eccentric Englishmen playing this odd music – people didn't know where to put it'. Despite massively increased sales, one of the problems he identified with the North American market, was the fractured nature of radio stations: 'You have this ridiculous radio format thing in which only certain kinds of music will be played on certain types of radio stations'.

In Steven's eyes, the record company weren't completely blameless. He told Dave Everley that Lava at one point sent out three different singles to different radio stations at the same time (perhaps in an effort to address the above-mentioned problem), but the result was only to 'disperse focus'.

If the new relationship didn't quite provide the desired sales levels, it did allow Porcupine Tree to reach a new level of recording quality; although Steven had been able to achieve excellent results in his home studio. For the first time, the band had access to a world-class and world-famous studio, The Power Station: opened in 1977, since with a name change to Avatar and back again. The studio has entertained clients including Nile Rodgers and Chic, Bruce Springsteen, Madonna, Lady Gaga, Bruno Mars, Paul McCartney and The Rolling Stones.

The studio engineer was Paul Northfield, who'd just finished recording *Vapor Trails* by Canadian rock band, Rush. Although Steven was able to make convincing song demos in his home studio, he told Bryan Reesman of *MixOnline.com* in April 2003 that the main difference between No Man's Land and Avatar, was 'the physical space available and the selection of microphones that a studio facility has ... it was really about the space and the atmosphere ... Plus, having Paul available'. Northfield and Wilson re-recorded the drums, bass, and most of the guitar parts from Steven's demos. Unusually, most of Steven's vocals were retained from the demos.

In a period of around three and a half weeks at Avatar, the band recorded no fewer than sixteen tracks: twelve of which appeared on the final album. Steven told Bryan Reesman: 'The reason it was so quick, was that the arrangements were very much mapped out. I just feel comfortable working that way, not (making) such a journey into the unknown, which kind of scares me.'

On Twitter, Steven described the album as the beginning of a new sound world for the band: 'What's interesting to me about *In Absentia*, is that you can hear how the sound we got on this album, defined our sound from here until our last album; I think we kind of arrived at the perfect combination of elements.'

In addition to the recording quality, the guitar sounds and heavy metal elements particularly characterised the new sound, becoming an essential part of the new style and taking the band into the world of progressive metal. Steven had grown up listening to the new wave of British heavy metal groups that appeared in the late 1970s and early 1980s: including bands like Iron Maiden, Def Leppard, Motörhead and Saxon. The movement spawned its own magazine – *Kerrang!* – which in turn created the verb 'to kerrang', meaning to play a distorted power chord on a guitar.

After falling out of love with heavy metal, Steven moved away from it but returned later when he realised that some of the most interesting, innovative music was being created within the extreme metal genre. As he told Dave Everley: 'For years I had been bemoaning the fact that no-one was experimenting in rock music anymore. When I was introduced to bands like Opeth and Meshuggah, I went, 'Ah, *this* is where the innovation is happening, at the brutal end of metal.''

Steven immediately saw how he could incorporate metal riffs into the band's style whilst retaining the melodic pop/rock elements, multi-layered harmonies, progressive rock song structures and high musicianship levels. Add to that, his ability to tell a story or create a mood within each song and across a whole album, and you have a sense of what made Porcupine Tree unique.

The other important aspect to the album's sound is Richard Barbieri's subtle keyboard work and soundscaping, which lifts and enriches the record. Steven told Bryan Reesman that he left Richard to add his own keyboard parts: 'One thing I don't try to do much within the demos is keyboards, because I can't possibly hope to come up with the sounds that Richard can.' Steven said he was proud of the fact that no digital keyboards were used at all – they were all analogue, including such classics as a Hammond organ, Mellotron, Fender Rhodes, and analogue synths such as the Prophet-5 and Roland System 700. As Steven said: 'I do think that gives the record a more organic, and hopefully, more timeless quality. It's not going to date in the same way that digital instrumentation tends to date records.'

All music and lyrics and by Steven Wilson except where marked.

'Blackest Eyes' (4:23)
One of Steven Wilson's great strengths as a lyricist is there are many equally valid ways of explaining what the lyrics mean. They're often poetic in the sense that they create vivid images in the listener's mind, without being specific. His lyrics also share with some of the great poetry, the power of concision, and describing emotions and images in a few perfectly crafted words. This doesn't mean they're meant to be read separately as poetry – the music provides a soundtrack to the words, often illuminating them, but sometimes providing a commentary deliberately at odds with their meaning. This song is a perfect example of this.

The serial killer theme is immediately introduced. The lyrics skilfully begin in the third-person, describing the killer's origins in two lines: 'A mother sings a lullaby to a child/Sometime in the future, the boy goes wild.'

The viewpoint then moves to that of the killer himself, and we spend the rest of the song inside his dark, twisted mind. The romantic imagery of a walk in the woods is combined with a romantic movie trope: a woman's makeup running when she cries – 'It's so erotic when your make-up runs.' But it's clear the killer is trying 'something under the trees' that's violent rather than romantic. The whispers echoing the words 'It's so erotic' add a sinister edge – the woman won't find the experience even remotely erotic.

We naturally feel revulsion at the killer, but Steven wants us to get inside his psyche. The chorus is almost jaunty, drawing the listener in, with a degree of self-awareness on the killer's part: 'I got wiring loose inside my head.' Is he trying to justify his actions or plead the defence of insanity? The words, 'Swim with me into your blackest eyes' are enticing; drawing the listener in with John Wesley's gorgeous harmony vocals. The killer's seductive words are presumably also designed to draw in his victim: he's inviting her to swim with him into 'your' (i.e. her) blackest eyes. This is open to interpretation: her eyes could be 'blackest', because of the killer's deepest, darkest twisted fantasies; or her eyes could appear dead to the killer (like the eyes on the album covers) because he doesn't recognise her as a living person, or her pupils could've dilated as they do at the moment of death.

This track was crucial in the band's history. It's the first song that potential new drummer, Gavin Harrison, played in rehearsal in England before travelling to New York to record the album. As Steven told Lasse Hoile: 'I made Richard and Gavin book a rehearsal studio so that Gavin could play through the songs. This was about a week before we were due to go to America. If that hadn't gone well, it would have been a disaster.' (References in this chapter to interviews with Lasse Hoile are from his fascinating documentary film *The Making of In Absentia*, part of the *In Absentia* deluxe edition of 2020).

In the Twitter Listening Party in July 2020, Steven said, 'Once he finished his first run-through, I knew immediately that he was a perfect fit for the band. Gavin was so powerful, and hit the drums so hard, but without any sense of losing finesse or control.'

This was the last song Steven wrote for the album. He said on the 2020 Twitter Listening Party: 'I wanted the opener to have a little of everything to come: the heavy riffs, the melodic song element, and the ambient textures, so it's all here.'

The track begins with a statement of Steven's new intent: a riff in drop-D tuning (a technique mentioned earlier). Steven told Lasse Hoile, 'it's one of the dumbest, most obvious examples of that'. He said the riff was 'a good one in that particular genre, and it's fun to play live'. He is being modest here – it's one of the most exciting riffs he has written.

'Trains' (5:56)

After the opening track's psychological and physical onslaught, there's a change of tone to a song about nostalgia. Steven told Lasse Hoile: 'Maybe people can't relate so much to serial killers ... but everyone can relate to a song about nostalgia for childhood.' 'Trains' is one of the band's most popular songs, but then, so is 'Blackest Eyes': showing that listeners can relate to songs on both topics.

Steven grew up within a short distance of a railway station and fell asleep each night to the sound of trains. The evocative sound still causes a Pavlovian response in him: 'When I hear it, I am instantly transported back to my childhood.'

The song immediately evokes a train set seen through a window. On his birthday in 2019, Steven posted an image of himself on Instagram with the caption, 'Here I am playing with one of my amazing presents, like the six-year-old that I was when I first got a train set for my birthday all those years ago, from my parents'. If you look at the image carefully, you can see the box bears the Hornby label: the iconic British brand.

Further nostalgic images evoked the summers of childhood – a time Steven described on the 2020 Twitter Listening Party:

> Those formative seasons when the sun's hang-time, stretches long into the evenings and bedtimes are delayed ... A time of very little responsibility, wonderment and discovery. A time of innocence and naivety. You will never have those first experiences again – your first kiss.

The song links what may have been two childhood memories: 'When I hear the engine pass/I'm kissing you wide.'

The engine is described as 'a 60-ton angel' and 'a pile of old metal' that falls to earth. This has led some online commentators to speculate that the angel is malevolent in some way – a dark angel that fell from heaven – but it's probably a metaphor for the engine speeding through the countryside in 'a radiant blur'. But elsewhere in the song, there's further evidence of a darker side, in the lines, 'You're tying me up/I'm dying of love'. These lines evoke the agonies of first love, to which the narrator is resigned: 'It's ok.'

This song is very different from the previous track. There are no drop-D distorted guitars. It begins with strummed acoustic guitars with a folky feel, accentuated through the beautifully layered wordless vocals that appear around three minutes in. There's an even more folky section where handclaps accompany a solo banjo, evoking an English barn dance or Morris dancers. Richard Barbieri wryly told Lasse Hoile: 'I didn't really like the middle section. The handclapping made me think of *Riverdance*.'

The band had reservations about the song in general; they didn't even play it on the album's first tour. Steven told Lasse Hoile: 'It's a good song, but I don't even think it's the best song on the record ... but most people would disagree with me.' Audience pressure led to the band performing it live, and on Spotify (as of August 2021), it's become Porcupine Tree's most-streamed song by a significant margin. Despite Richard and Steven's reservations, there are strong melodic elements, and a real sense of urgency in addition to its folk elements and an authenticity in the slightly raw and unpolished vocals. As Steven told Lasse Hoile: 'The fans can tell you what are the good songs.'

'Lips of Ashes' (4:39)

This track opens with Steven playing a hammered dulcimer: an instrument combining percussion and strings, similar to a piano mechanism. The dulcimer strings are stretched across a small soundboard, and the player hits the strings with hammers. Steven said on the 2020 Twitter Listening Party that the dulcimer part of the song 'started life as a piece titled '43553e99.01' from my ambient/textural side project Bass Communion'. That piece's enigmatic title was replaced with the equally mysterious 'Lips of Ashes'. It's not on Steven's list of serial killer songs, and Richard Barbieri rightly describes it as a beautiful piece, although he's talking more about the sound world than the lyrics.

Steven's more than capable of writing beautiful songs on gruesome subjects, and this may be one of them. The title suggests death and decay, as does the reference to paralysis and the 'crashing' of a blue vein. The black eyes imagery appears again; this time they're 'fading', again suggesting death. There are ambiguous references to touching the song's addressee 'inside' and drilling down inside.

In this album's track 'Strip the Soul', there's explicit and horrific sexual imagery, but here it could be metaphorical: the protagonist could be drilling down inside himself, touching the song's addressee emotionally. It's probably deliberately enigmatic.

The opening hammered dulcimer is drenched in echo, sounding initially like bells crashing from the sky – like the previous song's '60-ton angel'. At first, it seems like church bells pealing, linking to the previous song's nostalgia, but when the dulcimer continues playing it very quickly becomes clear that this is not the case.

Steven said on Twitter: 'This song basically appears on the album as my demo.' It does have the feeling of a solo album song. Richard Barbieri told Lasse Hoile that he added 'lots of textures to it', but that the main sound for him was 'this dulcimer thing that Steve played'.

'The Sound of Muzak' (4:59)

This music industry critique is something Steven Wilson attempted (with less success, as he himself later admitted) on 'Four Chords That Made a Million' from *Lightbulb Sun*. He laments the fact that music has become less significant in young people's lives than it used to be when he was growing up, and he later said that, if anything, things have gotten worse over the years. In 2019, Colin Edwin told Lasse Hoile that at the time he 'didn't really think it was worthy of ranting about ... but it's definitely come true, it's actually quite prophetic of him'. In the song, Steven sarcastically notes that 'The music of rebellion/Makes you want to rage/But it's made by millionaires/ Who are nearly twice your age.' Steven's prediction that in the future, music will not be designed to entertain, but only to 'repress and neutralize your brain', is bleak. But the fact that 'The Sound of Muzak' is so well written and performed, perhaps gives some hope. The song has become what Steven himself described as, a Porcupine Tree standard – one of their most popular songs.

The time signature is unusual, with seven beats to the bar: like the verse of Pink Floyd's 'Money'. Steven said on Twitter: 'It's great to be able to create an infectious groove that's in an unconventional time signature, but that doesn't sound *clever* or unnatural.' The 7/8 rhythm is made to feel more complex still, through Gavin Harrison's deliciously offbeat drumming; Colin Edwin's chorus bass line, which is busy but not overbearing; and the delightfully syncopated guitar solo.

'Gravity Eyelids' (7:56)

Another song about eyes. Interpretations have included necrophilia, child molestation, and having sex with a blow-up doll. Steven Wilson explained on Twitter: 'Lyrically, this is really about sexual tension, and I leave the rest to your imagination!'

This tension is perfectly illustrated through the icy introduction, with its spectral Mellotron choir and coldly mechanical electronic drums, giving a sense of the alienation between the protagonist and the addressee. The vocal is almost wistful, as if the protagonist is giving up on the prospect of sex: 'I've been waiting for hours/Let the salt flow, feel my coil unwind.' Steven summed up the mood: ''Gravity Eyelids' has a distinctly chilly vibe, thanks to its scratch-and-hiss programmed rhythm, and a ghost-choir effect. Definite trip hop influence here.'

But the trip hop doesn't remain throughout. Over the song's fairly expansive eight minutes, there's time to move in other directions and combine different styles. As Steven said, 'Again, it's a mixture of the three elements of heaviness, melodism [sic] and ambient textures.'

For the first two and a half minutes, the song hints at Steven's coming solo career; such as his first solo album, *Insurgentes* (2008), which has a similar feel on tracks like 'Abandoner' with its trip hop vibe. But the other band members do start to assert themselves at this point, with Gavin Harrison adding live drums to the programmed drums, and Colin Edwin appearing on bass. At around 3:40, Richard Barbieri, unusually, plays a keyboard solo. Normally his Porcupine Tree work is confined to rich, atmospheric textures; but this section highlights his modest, subtle, but very effective, style. The notes are simple – unlike the thrilling virtuosity of keyboard players like Rick Wakeman, Keith Emerson or Jon Lord – but equally powerful.

With Richard's solo in full flight, heavy metal guitars stir, followed by a full onslaught of the 'heaviness' Steven described. About six minutes in, earlier melodic sections return, and the song falls back into the icy, ambient trip hop textures it began with: a bleak reminder of the subject matter.

'Wedding Nails' (Steven Wilson, Richard Barbieri) (6:33)

Richard Barbieri had written the middle section of this instrumental, and Steven took it up from there. Even though there are no lyrics, it can still be classified as one of the album's serial killer songs. It's very noisy, almost as if to hide the victims' screams. If that seems fanciful, Steven and Richard's comments about the song's ending of the song are informative. On Twitter, Steven said: 'For the end, we wanted to create a stifling atmosphere, conveyed with chains and scraping piano strings. I think that's our serial killer again!'

Richard told Lasse Hoile that he 'tried to take the sound into the cellar and make it very dark ... a very kind of burial type thing'.

The song was a challenge for Gavin Harrison, as he told Lasse Hoile because he'd 'never played such heavy music before, at least in metal style music'. He played 'quite heavy punk' as Iggy Pop's drummer in the 1980s, but this was different: and in particular, hard to play live due to the amount of energy, stamina and concentration required.

The song is based around a driving, pulsating riff on a single distorted heavy guitar, soon joined by a second guitar in unison, on the opposite side of the stereo spectrum: a common way of producing that visceral metallic thrill. There are many examples of this throughout the metal genre and on Porcupine Tree's later albums. When they played metal riffs live, John Wesley often doubled Steven's guitar parts.

'Prodigal' (5:32)

Steven said on Twitter that he thought 'Prodigal' was 'perhaps the weakest track on the album'. He regretted not including 'Drown With Me' instead (included on the 2020 Deluxe Edition of the album and now available on streaming services. For a review of this track, see the chapter on compilations and bonus tracks). One reason he came to dislike 'Prodigal' is he felt it owed too obvious a debt to Pink Floyd, but despite that, 'It's still quite a nice song'.

The song is about a 'lonely misfit' who suffers from depression and has tried religion, medication and drugs, but none have helped him. The lyric has some of the album's most memorable lines, beginning with, 'I spend my days with all my friends/They're the ones on whom my life depends.' This gives the listener hope that the protagonist is finding a way out of his depression, but these hopes are cruelly shattered when it becomes clear that his 'friends' are just characters in a TV show: 'I'm gonna miss them when the series ends.' The image is a powerful one, that seems to have particular resonance for Steven. It re-appears later on this album, in 'The Creator Has a Mastertape': where the killer 'captured and collected things' to put in his shed, and raised 'a proper family' so he could 'tie them to a bed', treating them as if they were objects rather than real people. The lonely killer/collector appears again in 'Index' – from Steven's second solo album *Grace for Drowning* (2011) – which includes the lonely collector's chilling spoken lines: 'If I collected you and put you in a little cage/I could take you out and study you every day.'

Although 'Prodigal' is not specifically about a killer, it seems to have close links to songs demonstrating Steven's attempt to understand the psyche of those who are unable to relate normally to other human beings.

The track demonstrates the rhythmic subtlety of new drummer, Gavin Harrison. In addition to being a powerful drummer, Gavin's done a lot of research into rhythm theory, having written various books, including *Rhythmic Illusions* (1998). As he told Lasse Hoile, in this track, he creates the 'rhythmic illusion' that the tempo has varied, or that 'you've slowed down or sped up in a weird amount', even though nothing has actually changed. Drummer Bill Bruford used the technique on tracks like 'Sex Sleep Eat Drink Dream' – from King Crimson's *THRAK* (1995) – on which, at one point, time seems to be running backwards, as he offsets his drumming against that of fellow percussionist on the track, Pat Mastelotto.

'.3' (5:25)

This track began life as the middle section of 'Strip the Soul' and was given the title perhaps because it was a third of the original song. The two sections were reunited on the 2010 live album, *Anesthetize,* under the title 'Strip the Soul/ Dot Three'.

The track is almost entirely instrumental, apart from the enigmatic couplet: 'Black the sky, weapons fly/Lay them waste for your race.'

It's possible the title refers to World War III, but the most ingenious meaning suggestion comes from someone on songmeanings.com called mb1122, who in 2009 came up with the following theory: '.3 = 3/10 3/10 = 3:10 ... as in 2 Peter 3:10.' If you go to that chapter of the King James *Bible*, you'll find the following: 'But the day of the Lord will come as a thief in the night; in the which the heavens shall pass away with a great noise, and the elements shall melt with fervent heat, the earth also and the works that are therein shall be burned up.'

This apocalyptic end to the earth fits the lyrics very well, although it doesn't appear that Steven made the connection.

'The Creator Has a Mastertape' (5:21)

According to Steven Wilson in Twitter listening party, this title comes from two sources: the first being a reference to 'The Creator Has A Master Plan' by the American saxophonist, Pharoah Sanders, from his 1969 album *Karma*. The second refers to Jimi Hendrix leaving the *Axis: Bold as Love* master tape in a taxi, which meant that side one had to be remixed. The missing tape has never been recovered.

This is another of the album's serial killer songs. This time – as alluded to above under 'Prodigal' – the protagonist appears to have raised a 'proper family', entirely for the purpose of abusing them: an utterly nightmarish idea. The lyric refers to him tying his family to the bed, implying that he sexually abused them. The fact they were physically abused, and even murdered, is made clear in the horrific line: 'Your sordid home is running red,' and the reference to 'pills and chloroform' used in his crimes. The lyrics hint at the physical aspects of the killer's actions that were so difficult that 'he worked himself into the ground', just as he probably worked his victims' bodies into the ground by burying them. But what motivated the killer to treat his family in such an inhuman way, also fascinates Steven.

The 'creator' of the title could refer to God, who has a divine plan or 'mastertape'. Ironically, in this case, the mastertape has been lost. The implication is that the killer has lost his conscience or the moral compass that would allow him to recognise his family as real people. Instead, he stares into 'a void': which is the absence of his moral sense – another absence that relates to the album title.

It's unclear exactly what's caused the killer to act this way, but the lack of a 'mastertape' in his head, implies he has a brain disorder, rather than that he's acting out of pure evil. Perhaps – like the killer in 'Blackest Eyes' – he has 'got wiring loose inside (his) head'. Or perhaps the spike that he's driven 'into his head' has caused a brain injury. Damage to the frontal lobes can cause personality changes, including an increased propensity to anger and violence, and loss of emotions and inhibitions.

On Twitter, Steven said the lyrics were 'inspired by a book I read about the serial killer couple Rosemary and Fred West'. That book was *Happy Like Murderers* (1998) by Gordon Burn. The Wests killed at least twelve young women and girls between 1967 and 1987, burying the remains of nine of them under their Gloucester home. Like Steven Wilson, Gordon Burn had no sympathy for the couple, but did attempt to uncover the cause; looking into their deprived rural upbringings and family backgrounds.

A spiky guitar line creates an immediate sense of unease. The bass joins in with a jerky riff, constantly repeating the tritone interval. The guitar scatters fractured riffs across the soundscape. When Steven's vocal enters, doubled by a distorted version – the quietly whispered doubling we heard in 'Blackest Eyes' has now become frantic. The following fierce guitar riff adopts the intro bass part, but seems unable to find the right upper note to land on, adding to the tension. The track then stutters, as if unable to face the horror being described. The distortion level increases until the track finally grinds to a halt.

'Heartattack in a Layby' (4:15)
On Twitter, Steven said this track was 'one of my favourite songs on the album'. Like many of his songs, it tells a moving and profound story in a short space of time, using a few precise details and well-chosen words: 'I like to compare it to

the heartfelt letter that was never sent; the unspoken 'I love you'. The theme of regret has surfaced in several of my songs over the years, most notably on my album, *Hand. Cannot. Erase*'.

The scene is set immediately: the layby from the song title: 'I pull off the road/East of Baldock and Ashford/Feeling for my cell/In the light from the dashboard.' We are there, with the driver in the car at night (just as we are at the start of 'The Incident' – from *The Incident* (2009) – 'At junction eight the traffic starts to slow'). We can even hear the traffic going past at the beginning and can detect 'the smell of the rain in the air con'. The protagonist becomes increasingly unwell: 'Don't feel too good ... can't breathe too well ... I just need to lie down.' What he doesn't realise – but which slowly dawns on the listener – is that he's dying of a heart attack and will never return home. He's had an argument with his wife or partner waiting at home for him, and he regrets that this argument hasn't been resolved. Sadly, it never will be – she will never have the chance to apologise: 'She's waiting to make up/To tell me she's sorry/And how much she missed me.'

Steven told Lasse Hoile, the song originally started off 'with full drums and a heavy riff', but became 'a stripped-down ballad'. It was the right decision, as drummer Gavin Harrison graciously confirmed, although he hardly plays on the song: 'I think it's a beautiful song ... I like the lyrics and the composition, and it's quite powerful.'

This beautiful, poignant song ends with gorgeous multi-layered vocals – recorded in Steven's home studio – which include the desperately sad words, 'We'll grow old together'. We hear the traffic continuing to pass the layby, oblivious to the tragedy that has just occurred.

'Strip the Soul' (Steven Wilson, Colin Edwin) (7:21)

This final serial killer song is, in some ways, the most difficult to discuss, as it has some of the album's most explicit lyrics. The official video didn't help, which Steven described on Twitter as being 'quite a nasty piece, which I don't think anyone really liked or felt comfortable with. Alas, it was the only proper video we made for *In Absentia*.'

The inspiration is, again, serial killers Fred and Rose West. But there's a real sense of revulsion here, and less of an attempt to get inside the killers' minds in search of their motivations. We see the male protagonist's horrifying arrogance: he seems to have had children only in order to abuse them – like the killer in 'The Creator Has a Mastertape' – 'Raise the kids good, beat the kids good and tie them up'. He seems to have lost all human empathy – people are no longer sentient beings, but something for him to play with: 'This machine/Is there to please.'

The arrangement's supremely uncomfortable atmosphere transforms the song into something darkly poetic rather than entirely prurient. Colin Edwin wrote the chorus bass line, and Steven said on Twitter that he 'worked out some other sections to put around it, including the verse groove that opens the song'. This opening bass line has a similar feel to that of Massive Attack's *Blue*

Lines track, 'Safe From Harm' (1991), which in turn was sampled from Billy Cobham's 'Stratus' (from *Spectrum*, 1973).

The guitar solo at around four minutes in is probably the most extreme that Steven ever recorded for Porcupine Tree; he described it as 'pretty unhinged, which suits the subject matter'.

From around 5:30, a grinding heavy metal anthem moves almost in slow motion. The song ends with feedback from a guitar leaning against an amplifier: a classic rock trope many live bands have used when leaving the stage – leaving the audience with pure noise. But the guitar is suddenly pulled away, relieving us of the contrasting feelings of horror at the subject matter and elation with the music.

'Collapse the Light Into Earth' (5:49)

The final track differs completely in tone and theme from the rest of the album. Steven Wilson said during the Twitter listening party: 'This is my 9/11 song. It's not literal, as it's a break-up song, really, but there's something about it that will always be imbued with the sadness and grief of that tragedy for me. It was written in the days after.'

Like many millions of people across the world, Steven can remember where he was and what he was doing when the terrible events of 9/11 occurred; just as, for an earlier generation, the day in November 1963 when President Kennedy was shot, is frozen in time. On 11 September 2001, Steven was at home in his studio, working on a song. When he heard about the terrorist attacks in America, he abandoned that song, and two days later, started working on 'Collapse the Light Into Earth'.

Many composers responded to 9/11: including Steve Reich, Howard Goodall and John Adams. Some of the music composed relates directly to the tragedy. For instance, John Adams' *On the Transmigration of Souls* (2002) includes recordings of friends and family members of victims, reading out their names. Steve Reich's 'WTC 9/11' for string quartet and pre-recorded tape incorporates air traffic controller recordings and fragments of interviews with people who lived in Manhattan at the time of the attacks. Steven said of his own song: 'It's like William Basinski's *Disintegration Loops*. It's got nothing to do with 9/11, but there's a quality in that music which somehow connects with that time and that event.'

Basinski recorded his album using analogue tapes he'd been trying to digitise. He found that the magnetised metal was coming off the tapes, and each time he ran them over the tape heads, they disintegrated even more. He was just finishing the album when the 9/11 attack happened – he saw the terrifying events unfold from his Brooklyn rooftop. He dedicated the album to the 9/11 victims, and in 2011, a live orchestra performed it at New York's Metropolitan Museum of Art to mark the tenth anniversary of the attacks.

Steven Wilson's track shares the simple, austere, repetitive quality of the Basinski piece. 'Collapse the Light Into Earth' is effectively a solo piece, although Steven said he thought Richard Barbieri added a synth bass part. Opening and closing with the simplest of piano motifs, the strings and harmonies become richer as the song progresses. It's a beautiful, elegiac way to end the album.

Deadwing (2005)

Personnel:
Steven Wilson: vocals, guitar, piano, keyboards, hammered dulcimer, bass
Richard Barbieri: keyboards and synthesizers
Colin Edwin: bass
Gavin Harrison: drums and percussion
Mikael Åkerfeldt (Opeth): backing vocals; second guitar solo on 'Arriving
Somewhere But Not Here'
Adrian Belew (King Crimson): solo guitar on 'Deadwing' and 'Halo'
Recorded at No Man's Land, The Artillery, Bourne Place, New Rising, RAK, Astoria,
and Livingstone – March to October 2004
Produced and mixed by Steven Wilson
Release date: March 2005
Chart placings: UK: 97, USA: 132
Running time: 59:35 (Europe/Original edition); 64:34 (US edition)
Record label: Lava (Atlantic)
Current release: Kscope
Awards: 2005 Surround Music Awards 'Best Made for Surround Title'; Voted best
album of 2005 by readers of *Classic Rock* magazine; One of the ten best prog
albums of the first decade of the 21st century (*Classic Rock* magazine, February
2010)

Deadwing is the eighth Porcupine Tree studio album. Steven Wilson has
a passion for film and has often said he'd like to write film music. Bearing
in mind his ability to create powerful song images and stories, it's perhaps
surprising that (at the time of writing) he's not been asked to write a film score.

One way of ensuring you can write film music is to write and produce your
own film and provide your own music. In 2004, Steven and film director,
Mike Bennion (who had provided artwork and video materials for the early
Porcupine Tree albums), wrote a film script called *Deadwing*. In order to sell it
to potential financiers – and to generate public interest – they set up a Myspace
microsite which included the script's first fifteen pages. The site asked for
members of the public to post their comments: 'good or bad'.

The site stated that the proposed film's influences were the directors, David
Lynch, Nicolas Roeg and Stanley Kubrick, and the short pitch described the
project as '*Don't Look Now* meets *Mulholland Drive*'. This immediately
suggests the film to be an art-house thriller, possibly with surreal or
supernatural elements. Nicolas Roeg's *Don't Look Now* (1973) could be
described as a supernatural horror film; David Lynch's *Mulholland Drive*
(2001) is a surreal mystery.

The *Deadwing* microsite also provides a more detailed pitch:

David is a loner, submersed in his job as a sound designer. Late one night, he
spots something in the film rushes that he cannot explain. This event – and a

chance encounter with the mysterious Elizabeth – leads him down the winding path of his subconscious, where he has to confront his past, head on.

Despite the fact that the microsite generated a lot of public interest, Steven and Mike were unable to get film funding. Steven used some of the music he'd written for the film, on the *Deadwing* album, and also on his 2008 solo album, *Insurgentes*.

The film remains of interest to the extent it may reveal the album concept. According to several online sources, the songs 'Deadwing', 'Lazarus', 'Arriving Somewhere But Not Here', 'Mellotron Scratch' and 'Open Car' were written for the film. Ironically, one of the songs – 'Shallow' – has been used on a soundtrack: the 2005 crime drama, *Four Brothers*.

In an interview with MarBelle for the podcast *Directors Notes* in 2006, Mike Bennion was reluctant to explain the film plot in any more detail. He said he'd worked with Lasse Hoile on choosing the album booklet photographs, using the script as a starting point – he and Lasse 'tried to give visual clues in the booklet, but not really give any of the game away'. This causes a potential difficulty for the listener, as it's very difficult to establish exactly what the story is, but this doesn't take away from the visceral power many of the tracks possess – even those apparently not linked to the *Deadwing* film concept. Furthermore, it seems that the full film script is unlikely to have a clear linear narrative, delving deep into the character David's psyche, and into his past.

Even after the album release, Steven and Mike didn't give up on the project. In 2010 Steven told Anil Prasad of *Innerviews.org*:

> We keep showing it to anyone that will read it, but it's very hard to get someone to give you a million dollars to make a movie, particularly one that's very uncommercial and written by people who have never written a script before. That's why I took the pragmatic step of making a film about the making of my first solo record, *Insurgentes*. Lasse Hoile came out with me, and we made this surreal road movie that's much more than a documentary.

In 2020, the project re-appeared under a different title: *And No Birds Sing*. Steven and Mike had reworked the script, but it still featured David, the sound designer, as the central character. In September that year, a short 'teaser' was released on YouTube, filmed using amateur actors (including a short cameo from Steven himself), directed by Mike Bennion, with sound design by Steven. On his website, Steven said he hoped the complete film would go into full production in 2021, but in the meantime, gave this teasing description:

> It's a story that crosses genres, having aspects of psychological thriller, horror and mystery. Reality merges with film and the supernatural when a London director starts to experience strange events and is forced to confront

his troubled past. The film blurs the lines of reality, memory and fiction, where sound constantly motivates the twists and turns of the action.

Only fifteen pages of the script were ever publicly released, so it's difficult to work out exactly what the film's about and how it relates to the album lyrics. To summarise what we learn from the script:

It begins with a young woman singing a lullaby to a three-year-old boy. She blows out the candles in his bedroom, leaving the light of the full moon flooding in. The scene switches to the boy running through a wood by the light of the full moon from the last scene. He wears a nightshirt, and his feet are bare.

We cut to a vagrant, lighting a fire on waste ground; the scene is repeated a few times, and it becomes clear that David – a sound designer – is editing it in a video editing suite. The boy we saw in the first two scenes, suddenly appears in the video David's editing, and to his horror, disappears again when he replays the video.

David leaves work, and goes to catch the Underground home. He walks through the remnants of a fruit market, passing a group of young people with collection boxes, wearing costumes and papier-mâché heads. He steps onto the train, with his headphones on, and we hear what he hears through a small microphone he's using to record sound effects and the speech of others in the carriage. A vagrant sleeps at the end of the carriage. David walks home through a park and sees strange words and images chalked on the paving stones: similar to the work of painter and poet, William Blake. David returns to his small one-bedroom bachelor flat, where clanking noises come from the pipes, and an Italian couple make love noisily in the flat above.

The next day, David returns to the studio, and inserts the clanking sound into the film soundtrack he's working on, much to the confusion of the director. Eventually, the director accepts that the sound works, and even suggests that David should reshoot some of the video, as well as sound design.

At the Tube station on the way home that night, David sees an advert for a child-abuse charity, with the image of a small boy saying the 'monster' comes at night. David meets Elizabeth – a young woman in her late twenties, with a long red coat and red high heels – who is terrified of a man who seems to be following her. She joins David in his carriage, seeking his protection from the terrifying man.

The album won Best Made for Surround Title in the 2005 Surround Music Awards. Steven has been working with surround sound for many years: initially with Elliot Scheiner, on the 5.1 mixes of *In Absentia* and *Deadwing;* then moving into remixing classic albums in surround sound for other artists.

The band's next album – *Fear of a Blank Planet* – was nominated for a 2007 Grammy award for Best Surround Sound Album. The limited-edition deluxe

box set of Steven's sixth solo album – *The Future Bites* – released in early 2021, not only included standard 5.1 mixes but also – for the first time – mixes in Dolby Atmos. This technology provides multiple point sources, rather than just the five, adding height, so that sounds also come from above and below the listener. Steven's tour to promote his *To the Bone* album used surround sound, which worked particularly well in London's Royal Albert Hall due to the venue's roundness.

All music and lyrics by Steven Wilson except where marked.

'Deadwing' (9:46)

In the title track, presumably one of the bird's wings is broken: like the bird in The Beatles' 'Blackbird' (from *The Beatles* (1968)). Yet, unlike in 'Blackbird', there's no attempt to persuade the bird to fly. Instead, 'Deadwing' is a surreal collection of fragmented imagery, some of which relates to the film's ghost story, although it's unclear how much of it comes from the script. The spoken references to the 'voices through the floor' could refer to the Italian lovers in the flat above David; and the 'high heeled shoes' to the red shoes Elizabeth wears when they first meet. The train near the song's end could be the Tube train in which Elizabeth joins David. The 'yellow windows of the evening train' is a memorable image: one that Steven returned to on *The Incident*, providing a song title.

The album starts with an unusual, pulsing synth line, which fierce guitar chords soon disrupt. It's a compelling opening, urgently throwing the listener straight into the ghost story, rather than building up the tension slowly as often happens: 'And something warm and soft just passed through here/It took the precious things that I hold dearer.' Starting the lyrics with the word 'and', suggests we've come in halfway through the story – we're immediately intrigued to learn what's just happened. Even the guitar chords seem somehow unsettled, uneasy, and incomplete, like a half-thought.

The following drop-D guitar riff shows we're back in the progressive metal of *In Absentia*. The riff is built around a simple octave leap but rumbles uneasily around the bottom note. An even fiercer riff appears around three minutes in, before some characteristically rich harmonies gently express the frightening thought that 'You are on closed-circuit TV'. At around five minutes in, there's yet another – this time grand and anthemic – riff, before the music falls away into dark, ghostly introspection: perhaps illustrating the 'spectre from the next life' that appears breathing fog on the train window.

Mikael Åkerfeldt from Swedish progressive metal band, Opeth, came in to do backing vocals on 'Deadwing', 'Lazarus' and 'Arriving Somewhere But Not Here'. He also recites the ghostly spoken-word inserts, where he rhythmically speaks – almost whispers – some of the album's darkest lyrics, such as 'Like a cancer scare/In a dentist's chair.'

Chris Maitland's departure had meant there was a backing vocalist vacancy. Steven told Martien Koolen and Bart Jan Van der Vorst of *DPRP.net* in 2008: 'Gavin replaced Chris, and Chris was the only other singer in the band, so there's been a need to have other vocal textures to join with my vocals to make harmonies.'

John Wesley sang backing vocals on *In Absentia* and live on tour, but Steven was keen to use Mikael on this album: 'We have always worked very well together, because I worked with him on his records, so I always knew I would want to have him on one of my records one day.' To date, the two artists have collaborated on one album: *Storm Corrosion* (2012).

Another *Deadwing* guest musician is King Crimson's Adrian Belew, who plays the solos on 'Deadwing' and 'Halo'. Steven told Anil Prasad that he was very excited to hear from Adrian: Steven had grown up listening to King Crimson. Belew was a member from 1981 to 2013, playing on some of the band's best albums, including *Discipline* (1981) and *THRAK* (1995). Steven returned the favour by doing the surround sound mix on the *Discipline* 40th anniversary edition. Unfortunately, the two musicians were unable to meet – for logistical reasons – so Steven left gaps on the two *Deadwing* tracks, for Adrian's contributions:

> His playing was completely uncontrolled, in that there was no conception of what key the song is in, or what time signature you're supposed to be in. He didn't allow himself to be restricted by things like notes and rhythms. Afterwards, I sifted through and chose the bits that were most empathetic to the way I imagined the tracks.

As is to be expected from Adrian – considering his King Crimson work – the solo is fractured, dystopian and intense.

The track ends with the sound of someone walking along a train platform; perhaps Elizabeth in her high heels.

'Shallow' (4:16)

Steven Wilson described this song to Aidan Gray of *SMNNews.com* in March 2005 as, 'a big rock number, the closest Porcupine Tree has come to making a big dumb rock song'. Released as a single (radio edit) in the US, it spent eleven weeks in the *Billboard* Mainstream Rock Songs chart, peaking at number 26 in May 2005. In Europe, the single was 'Lazarus'. Steven told Aidan: 'The European affiliates felt it was too heavy for radio. They were right, there's no rock radio format in Europe as there is in America. They went with the mellow chilled out song, 'Lazarus'.'

The opening riff has all the swagger of Led Zeppelin's 'The Ocean', from *Houses of the Holy* (1973). A traumatic experience has severely damaged the song's protagonist: 'Did something in my past create a hole?' This has led him to have shallow, difficult relationships with other humans, particularly women. He's withdrawn from society, spending time on the internet instead: 'The millions pain me/It's easier to talk to my PC.' Steven would return to this theme in far more detail on *Fear of a Blank Planet*.

At around three minutes in, reversed vocals appear to say, 'After it, I guess I'll just die, you know', though it's hard to be sure.

'Lazarus' (4:18)

Lazarus is another song written for the *Deadwing* film. Again, it's unclear exactly how it relates to the film, but in some ways, what's more important, is that this beautiful piano-led ballad has deservedly become a fan favourite.

The chordal simplicity gives a timeless quality – like many of the best ballads – and the lyric's poetic quality strengthens it: 'Follow me down to the valley below/You know/Moonlight is bleeding from out of your soul.'

This appears to be sung by the mother of the film's central character, David: 'My David, don't you worry.' It may be that she's died, and the 'valley below' she refers to is 'the valley of the shadow of death' from Psalm 23. The song title strengthens the possible biblical reference; In the *Gospel of St John*, Jesus brought Lazarus back to life. The title took on a different resonance when David Bowie used it his last album *Blackstar* in 2016. Steven dedicated *his* 'Lazarus' to Bowie on his 2016 tour promoting *Hand. Cannot. Erase.*, pointing out that the song's character was also named David.

The track ends with the mother enticing David – here addressed as Lazarus, as if his return from the dead has only been temporary – to join her in death: 'Come to us, Lazarus/It's time for you to go.'

The final chord change is one of the most moving in all of Steven's songs, giving a sense of release and homecoming as David and his mother reunite.

The song was released as a single, though it didn't chart. The video includes many images of a boy's childhood, again touching on the nostalgia theme. This is sometimes linked with Steven's memories of hearing trains when he was growing up – as described under 'Trains' from the previous album. It's, therefore, not a great surprise to hear the sound of a train rattling along the track at the end.

'Halo' (Richard Barbieri, Colin Edwin, Gavin Harrison, Steven Wilson) (4:38)

After the previous song's complex imagery and allusive meanings, 'Halo' seems fairly straightforward. The theme is religion. The protagonist appears to be a born-again Christian. Steven is critical, not necessarily of religion itself here, but of the arrogant holier-than-thou attitude, as expressed in the lines 'I'm not the same as you/'Cause I've seen the light ... You can be right like me/We've got it all.'

Most major religions have used the halo in their iconography, so the reference may not be specifically Christian. The song's constant 'God' references imply a monotheistic religion, such as Christianity, Judaism or Islam.

The song features one of Colin Edwin's best bass lines, Steven's impassioned vocals, Gavin Harrison's powerful drumming and Barbieri's darkly dystopian synth line. Andrew Belew provides a short, frenzied guitar solo, adding to the atmosphere of claustrophobic paranoia and self-righteousness.

'Arriving Somewhere But Not Here' (12:02)

Another song written for the *Deadwing* film, and another fan favourite. This track has attracted a lot of online comments and many different interpretations, showing how ambiguous the lyrics are. Like many of the best Porcupine Tree songs, it's shot-through with melancholy existential thoughts; but the melody's beauty and the rich vocal harmonies – some by Mikael Åkerfeldt – are uplifting.

The narrator seems to address himself: with warnings, questions and statements – all of which lead to a failure to arrive where he'd expected to: which was certainly 'not here'.

The song begins with a series of warnings based on the protagonist's fear, jumping very quickly from the perhaps wise advice to not stop the car while driving at night to a much deeper fear: 'Never look for truth in your mother's eyes.' An optimistic interpretation could be that his mother is trying to protect her son from life's harsh reality. But it seems more likely – bearing in mind the overall depressing context – that the line implies he should avoid looking in his mother's eyes in case he sees hatred or indifference.

The narrator contemplates the violent death he may suffer, which, again, isn't what he'd planned: 'Did you imagine the final sound as a gun?/Or the smashing windscreen of the car?' He considers his failure in everything he's ever attempted: 'All my designs simplified/And all of my plans compromised/All of my dreams sacrificed.' He is stuck in an endless cycle of 'Drinking down the poison the way you were taught', failing to avoid the poisonous and destructive habits he learned in childhood: presumably from his mother. At the end, he asks himself if he feels torn apart through envy for other 'sons of mothers' who have had better lives.

The song begins with unusual synth textures. When the acoustic guitars enter, there's a feeling of stasis, of suspension in time, as the protagonist contemplates his existence. The deliberately lo-fi vocal production heightens this, adding to the sense of alienation and existential crisis. The echo starting on the words 'Did you imagine the final sound' draws us deeper into the protagonist's despair.

As with many of Steven's longer songs, the track has huge dynamic contrasts. A heavier, more metal riff – of the style the band adopted from *In Absentia* onwards – appears at around six minutes, taken to full onslaught by seven minutes in. The track could've easily ended on that visceral high, but instead, the main acoustic guitar riff returns, this time with an additional disturbing note that interferes with the established harmony.

A further quiet, spacey section with an almost trip hop vibe, features a limpid but mournful guitar solo from Mikael Åkerfeldt.

The song ends with the track's beginning main riff, in a long, slow instrumental fade, as if the protagonist has arrived back where he started, but not where he wanted to be.

The song title was used for the band's first live concert DVD, *Arriving Somewhere...*: recorded in 2005 at Park West in Chicago, with additional material from the German television show, *Rockpalast*.

'Mellotron Scratch' (6:56)

This song, also written for the film, refers to the main character breaking up with an un-named lover, due to their lack of communication: 'And I'm looking at a blank page now/Should have filled it up with words somehow ... I'd bear my soul, but she didn't hear.' There is a brief mention of happier times that have now gone: 'Well, maybe she remembers us collecting space up in the sky.' There is also a reference to a poignant memory: the way the sound of a Mellotron made her cry.

The Mellotron was an early form of sampler – a real instrument was recorded separately, with an analogue tape loop (with three different sounds on it) to match each note on the keyboard. But Mellotrons were expensive to build: in the 1960s, costing a significant portion of a house price. Ironically, one of the earliest digital samplers, the Fairlight CMI, was equally expensive. The song title may refer to the noise a Mellotron makes when it's not working properly. So the line 'The scratching of a Mellotron' doesn't really refer to the sound; it refers to any blatant sign that something's not working properly.

In September 2005, Steven told Mike Mettler of *soundandvision.com* that he was a huge Mellotron fan because, 'It has a scratchy, lo-fi sound, but it has a real character. The surface noise of old records – I love those sounds. There's something about them that just gives a certain grain to things.'

An alternative meaning could be the idea of something being put together quickly: like a scratch band of musicians. So a Mellotron scratch could refer to an early version of a song, laid down very quickly as a first thought. This ties in with the lyrics: 'And I'm looking at a blank page now/Should I fill it up with words somehow.' Appropriately enough, a Mellotron choir appears at this point, though generally, the instrument is used fairly sparsely in the track.

The song's most striking instrumental part (before the guitars kick in about two minutes from the end) is a piano theme, pivoting very simply from E major to C major, with a short rest in between, giving a sense of contemplative melancholy.

The rich backing vocals enhance the song's beauty. When the guitars appear, they howl briefly and metallically, before an insistent series of chords, end the song in a sea of beautifully overlaid vocals. The final brief a cappella section, has a similar feel to the beautiful 'Drag Ropes': from *Storm Corrosion* (2012).

'Open Car' (3:46)

This is the last of the *Deadwing* film songs. A woman is in an open convertible car in summer: 'Hair blown in an open car/Summer dress slips down her arm.' It's a sunny, vaguely erotic image, contrasting with the lyric's overall troubled message. It starts happily enough, with a simple description of the protagonist's lust: 'Nothing like this/Felt in her kiss/Cannot resist her.' But a vocal intensity suggests all is not well in the relationship: the vocals are chopped into short sections, delivered first to the listener's left ear, then the right, creating a restless feel. At the end of verse one, our fears are confirmed when it's revealed the relationship is an illicit affair: 'Here is the sin/Something to lie about.'

The song's other main image is a 'heart-shaped shell', which the narrator tries to hide, as it represents his true deep feelings for the woman. His heart is shattered, breaking inside his stomach. Resignedly, he lets the pieces 'lie just where they fell': a vivid and powerful heartbreak depiction. A quiet but telling aside shows the true nature of his emotions, despite his love for her: 'Being with you is hell.'

The heavy staccato guitar riff dominating the verses mirrors the narrator's anguish, and the memorable chorus is layered with the backing vocals that became such a Porcupine Tree signature.

The coda is unusual and effective: after the guitar's earlier fury, a gentle acoustic guitar shows the narrator has finally come to terms with the relationship; he looks back on the image of the woman in the open car, almost with nostalgia now.

'The Start of Something Beautiful' (Steven Wilson, Gavin Harrison) (7:39)

This is one of many Porcupine Tree songs about unrequited love. The bitter narrator thought the relationship with the woman he's addressing was going to be 'The Start of Something Beautiful', but was proven wrong. Despite the depth of his love for her, she prefers to remain 'good friends'. She has issues of her own, which may have caused her to push him away: 'Mother lost her looks for you/Father never wanted you'.

Some of the lyrics suggest the narrator's obsession with her is unhealthy. If this song had appeared on *In Absentia*, lines like 'I got your voice on tape/I got your spirit in a photograph' could be spoken by one of that record's obsessive lonely killers; and the line 'cold inside my arms you are' could refer to the woman's actual death, rather than her emotional withdrawal. But as with any art, context is crucial; although the line 'down inside my soul you are', does show the intensity of his unrequited love.

The track begins with atmospheric synth washes, Colin's superb bass line and Steven's intimate, plaintive vocals. In the chorus, his voice is slightly distorted, evoking the distance the character now feels between him and his former lover. The sour, almost trip hop drums of the long instrumental section beautifully express the alienation. This moves to a more hopeful piano-led section, where the protagonist reminisces about happier times: 'I remember when you took my hand and led me through the rain.'

The song being a co-write with drummer, Gavin Harrison, may partly explain the rhythmic complexity: switching between the time signatures of 9/8 in the verse and 5/8 in the chorus. This gives the track an uneven, syncopated feel, compared with most pop and rock songs, which are in the standard 4/4. Gavin included a big-band version of the song on his 2015 album, *Cheating the Polygraph*.

'Glass Arm Shattering' (Richard Barbieri, Colin Edwin, Gavin Harrison, Steven Wilson) (6:13)

The final track is one of the simplest ever Porcupine Tree songs, using the same three chords for most of the song. Like 'Collapse the Light Into Earth' from *In Absentia*, it's a quiet, contemplative track, after all the earlier turbulent emotions.

Lasse Hoile directed the video. As he says in his book, *Muzak: The Visual Art of Porcupine Tree*, when he heard the song, he visualised a 'floaty kinda thing' and decided to film two people swimming naked underwater in a swimming pool. He was upset that the woman in the video had her long hair cut short the day before the shoot: 'It would have looked dreamier if she had kept her hair long.' Lasse employed a skilled diver who was also a photographer and a safety diver. The shoot budget was only £900. The video mostly features the woman, but the man joins her at the end, kissing her tenderly. It seems that with the album's end, love has finally arrived: the last words of the song are 'Feeling all your love'.

The video begins with some scratchy artefacts imposed on it, giving it the feel of an old film. The music starts similarly, with a scratchy audio filter on the guitars. In a pleasing effect, the filter dissipates to reveal the full audio quality. Despite its simplicity, the song sustains interest for its full six minutes, through clever, sensitive production and quality musicianship – bringing the album to a tranquil close.

Fear of a Blank Planet (2007)

Personnel:
Steven Wilson: vocals, guitars, piano, keyboards
Richard Barbieri: keyboards, synthesizers
Colin Edwin: bass
Gavin Harrison: drums
Alex Lifeson (Rush): guitar solo on 'Anesthetize'
Robert Fripp (King Crimson): soundscapes on 'Way Out of Here'
John Wesley: backing vocals
London Session Orchestra
Recorded at No Man's Land, Bourne Place, New Rising, The Artillery, Nightspace,
Mark Angelo, Red Room Recorders, DGM: October-December 2006; Air studios
(Strings)
Produced and arranged by Porcupine Tree
Mixed and mastered by Steven Wilson
Highest chart places: UK: 31, USA: 59
Running time: 50:48
Awards: Grammy nomination: Best Surround Sound Album (2007); *Classic Rock*
magazine: Album of the Year (2007)
Release dates: UK: 16 April 2007; The rest of Europe and the US: 24 April 2007
Record label: Roadrunner (UK), Atlantic (USA)
Current release: Transmission

Fear of a Blank Planet is Porcupine Tree's ninth studio album. It takes its title
from Public Enemy's 1990 hip hop album, *Fear of a Black Planet*: an album
Steven Wilson admires greatly.

The term 'blank planet', expressed Steven's profound concern about the
effect that technology was having, particularly on teenagers, who he felt
were failing to connect with the real world as a result of their obsession with
computers, iPods, mobile phones and gaming platforms. When writing the
lyrics in 2006, Steven may have been unaware that smartphones and social
media were about to become ubiquitous. But his fears seem prescient, bearing
in mind, for instance, the 2020 Netflix docudrama, *The Social Dilemma*,
in which former major tech company employees make serious allegations
about social network monetisation and the dopamine hits that engaging with
them apparently brings. Steven told Cornelia Wickel of *Guest Musicalypse*
in November 2007 that he was as guilty as anyone of being too attached to
technology (although, in 2009, he did destroy several iPods to promote his first
solo album *Insurgentes*).

Steven said the Bret Easton Ellis novel *Lunar Park* strongly influenced the
album's theme of alienated teenagers. A character called Bret – partly based
on the author – narrates the novel, particularly in the book's first part, where
he describes his early successes as the author of *Less Than Zero* (1985) and
American Psycho (1991). The novel is a strange but weirdly compelling mix of

partly-imagined autobiography, fantasy, satire and horror. Steven was intrigued by the narrator's son Robby, who spends his time in his room, playing games and watching TV, or hanging out at the shopping mall with his equally vacuous friends. According to Steven's website:

> The lyrics deal with two typical neurobehavioural developmental disorders affecting teenagers in the 21st century: bipolar disorder and attention deficit disorder, and also with other common behaviour tendencies of youth, like escapism through prescription drugs, social alienation caused by technology, and a feeling of vacuity – a product of information overload by the mass media.

Lunar Park, mercilessly satirises parents' over-reliance on prescription drugs to control their children (and themselves), in a scene where a birthday party features six-year-olds so over-medicated that they move lethargically and speak monotonously, chewing their fingernails until they bleed; a paediatrician stands by in case further medical intervention is needed.

The album is written from the point of view of a teenage boy, slightly older than Robby is in the novel. This suggests a degree of empathy with the boy's existential blankness, whereas, in the novel, the narrative is written from the viewpoint of Robby's father Bret, who finds it almost impossible to communicate or to understand with his son.

The album lyrics are rather more earnest than satirical, although the odd turn of phrase expressing teenage angst, can be witty: 'Your mouth should be boarded up/Talking all day with nothing to say' from the title track; and 'I'm trying to forget you/And I know that I will/In a thousand years/Or maybe a week' from 'Way Out of Here'.

In interviews around the time of the album's release, Steven expressed deep disquiet with the effect of teenagers' access not just to drugs, but to guns: i.e. the massacres at Columbine (April 1999) and Virginia (April 2007). He also referred to violence and obsession linked with fame fostered by reality TV; and the shootings at Westroads Mall in Omaha, Nebraska (December 2007), where the gunman left a suicide note saying this would make him famous.

All this makes the album seem very serious and heavy, and in some ways, it is. But as with many great rock albums, the lyrics serve the music, which is a perfect example of Porcupine Tree's mature style. Steven said that Swedish progressive metal band Meshuggah strongly influenced him to write heavy riffs. But in an interview with Martien Koolen and Bart Jan Van der Vorst of *DPRP.net* in 2008 – titled 'Fear of a Dull Band' – there's an amusing discussion involving all four band members trying to decide exactly how heavy they'd become. Steven decides that even he is not sure: 'I think *Fear of a Blank Planet* gives the impression that it is heavy, because it starts with a long heavy song, and then there is 'Anesthetize', which has this long heavy section. But I don't know, you'd have to analyse it. 'My Ashes' is pretty mellow, as is the last section of 'Anesthetize'.'

Perhaps the best way to describe the music is a unique combination of heavy rock, melodic pop, art rock and heavy metal with classical strings and gorgeous vocal harmonies. The tag 'Progressive rock' doesn't really do it justice, except to the extent that it gives some idea of the ambitious scope and some of the song lengths. Talking to Joey Kelley of *Prog Archives* in April 2007, Steven said it was a progressive album in a different sense: 'Sometimes you have to confront your own patterns and expectations of yourself and do away with things that you enjoy doing in order to move forward and keep evolving as a musician. That's exactly the definition of the word 'progressive', of course.'

Steven also said that the term had been used to describe 'Genesis circa 1972 or King Crimson circa 1967', but that in his view, there was now a new breed of bands who'd changed the way people think about the word 'progressive': such as The Mars Volta, Tool, Opeth, The Flaming Lips, Sigur Ros, Isis, Mastodon, Radiohead, Muse, and Coheed and Cambria. Whether all those bands can be labelled as progressive is open to debate, but they share a sense of ambition and an attempt to push boundaries and reinvent genres.

In August 2009, two years after the album's release, Steven described it in a *FaceCulture* interview on YouTube, as the band's 'least commercial album ever' and said he made no attempt to write any songs that would be played on the radio. Despite his best efforts, *Fear of a Blank Planet* became, at that time, the band's most commercially successful album.

All music and lyrics by Steven Wilson, except where marked.

'Fear of a Blank Planet' (7:28)

The first track immediately establishes the album's theme, beginning with the sound of keys on a vintage computer. It's been suggested that the keyboard is typing the album title. Then comes a quick burst of an unidentified noise sample – probably from the TV which is 'always on', flickering in the corner of a teenage boy's bedroom. The opening acoustic guitar riff begins with a repeating octave interspersed with a tritone (an interval often used in heavy metal, as in the title song of Black Sabbath's eponymous 1970 debut). This suggests the song will be heavy, even though the guitar sound is clean. Later, distorted guitars play the riff as the song gains metallic momentum.

Gavin Harrison's drums enter in a syncopated rhythm, setting up the dystopian mood. Steven told *DPRP.net* that it was partly Gavin's presence that maintained the heavier sound, 'because Gavin is a very powerful drummer'.

Typical of Porcupine Tree, the heavy opening suddenly morphs into a beautiful moment of introspection, an instrumental at around four minutes in, still using the opening guitar riff, but with Richard Barbieri's atmospheric synth-playing and Gavin Harrison's languid drumming. It could represent the protagonist's state of mind, as the drugs drag him further from reality, or it could be a moment of sanctuary. Then comes a wonderfully sinuous metallic riff with a compelling sense of urgency and excitement: perhaps the boy's anger returning. It's this ability to meld several musical ideas, that demonstrates Porcupine Tree at their best; a less inventive band would've pursued just one of the elements relentlessly: perhaps creating a certain monolithic grandeur but lacking the subtlety of the songwriting here. The fact that Steven surrounded himself with virtuosos – all bringing their own different strengths – makes this musical statement even more forceful.

The song's driving urgency is paradoxically at odds with the lyrics, which often express the torpor of the teenage boy's life: 'I'm stoned in the mall again/Terminally bored/Shuffling 'round the stores.' The boredom is felt so keenly that it bursts out into a burning rage, perfectly capturing the teenager's hormonal maelstrom. This is combined with a cynical detachment and the sedative effect the prescription drugs have on him: 'My face is Mogadon ... I'm tuning out desires.' The heavy vocal compression heightens the effect in the verse, creating a sense of detachment. But behind the teenager's blank, cynical, sneering facade lies a frightened boy: 'How can I be sure I'm here?/The pills I'm taking confuse me.' The change to a warm and natural vocal sound gives a glimpse of the real human being.

One of the song's best lines shows another example of Steven's wry wit: 'Xbox is a god to me.' It was therefore not without irony that, in 2019, a video game developer featured the song in the closing credits of a game called Control. Being the gentleman that he is, Steven thanked the developers on Twitter in September 2019.

Long-term band collaborator, Lasse Hoile, directed the music video. It shows teenagers playing with guns, and was released in April 2007, unfortunately at the time of the Virginia Tech shooting. In the wake of the shooting, the video was temporarily taken down. The day of the massacre – 16 April – was also the UK album release date. A few days later, Steven expressed his concern in the interview with *Prog Archives*: 'I heard about the shootings in Virginia, and I'm thinking I hope this album isn't cursed, but the whole Columbine thing is wrapped up in the record.' The Columbine High School massacre was the subject of Michael Moore's Oscar-winning 2002 documentary, *Bowling for Columbine*.

'My Ashes' (Steven Wilson, Richard Barbieri) (5:07)

This song, co-written with the band's keyboard player, Richard Barbieri, begins, appropriately enough, with an electric piano through a Leslie speaker: which colours and humanises the sound, as vibrato can with a human voice or string instrument. After the opening track's fierce onslaught, 'My Ashes' brings a moment of contemplation and beauty.

But in keeping with the album's theme, the song is shot through with not only melancholy resignation, but also a degree of bitterness. The central character is presumably the teenage boy of the opening track: based on the *Lunar Park* character. In the novel, the relationship between the narrator Bret, and his son Bobby, is very strained: the boy blaming his problems on his parents: 'When a mother and father/Gave me their problems/I accepted them all.'

There is a further, more subtle, link with the novel. In the final chapter, Bret scatters his father's ashes, which has led some online commentators to suggest the song is a direct homage to the chapter or that it quotes heavily from it. In fact – although there is a strong link between the two – it's more elusive than that would suggest. The book's final section is a poetic tour de force; Bret's father's ashes rise and dance through the corridors of Bret's memory, above the landscapes of his past, drifting across the endless disappointments he suffered from his father. The song shares the book's poetic conceit of the ashes drifting across the sky, and falling 'over all the things we've said'. The song and the book even share the images of a piano keyboard and a little boy on a bike. But the song has a redemptive quality that the book is unable to reach – 'They go beyond the fog/And return to save the child that I forgot' – the implication being that the song's protagonist is able to save himself, whereas in the book, the fog envelops a disappearing family. At the chapter's end, Bret disappears into the book's pages, where he can always be found. In the same way, the song's protagonist disappears: trapped, as his ashes drop upon a park in Wales, where there are 'never-ending clouds of rain'. It feels like a specific reference to Steven Wilson's childhood, but like many good poets, he leaves the reference unexplained.

This is one of the band's simplest songs, consisting of a short instrumental introduction, two verses and two choruses; with plangent piano chords and the gorgeous strings orchestration of prog rock keyboard player Dave Stewart (not the Eurythmics member).

'Anesthetize' (17:42)

This track is of epic proportions and length; the longest Porcupine Tree album track since 'Moonloop' and the two-part title track from *The Sky Moves Sideways*, over ten years earlier. In 2017 the track was voted number 32 in *Prog* magazine's 100 Greatest Prog Anthems of All Time. A superb live version -recorded in Tilburg, Netherlands in October 2008 – is on the 2012 CD/DVD, *Anesthetize*. The DVD was *Classic Rock* magazine's DVD Release of the Year and was voted number 2 in *Prog Archives* Top DVD/Videos of All Time.

The track is divided into three sections: 'Anesthetize', 'The Pills I'm Taking' and 'Surfer'. The second section was named on the Octane Twisted live album, where it was joined with 'Russia on Ice'. Gavin Harrison confirmed all three titles in episode 61 of the *Kscope Podcast* presented by Billy Reeves in March 2015.

Part I: 'Anesthetize'

The opening words of the novel, *Lunar Park*, are almost identical to the song's opening words: 'A good impression of myself.' In the novel, its author, Bret Easton Ellis, quotes his wife (actress Jayne Dennis) telling him he does an 'awfully good' impression of himself. The context is Bret deciding to dress up as himself when the family go to a Halloween party. He devotes a good part of the book's first chapter to comparing these simple opening words to the openings of his previous novels, which had become increasingly complicated; chapter two begins with Jayne repeating these words. The problem with all this, is that Jayne Dennis never existed. She was a fictional character, though one that had her own website – www.jaynedennis.com (since taken down) – complete with fictional biography and filmography. Steven Wilson was not, of course, averse to invented characters: as we know from earlier in this book, Porcupine Tree itself was originally a fictitious band, complete with a fictional biography and discography. No doubt there would've been a website for the fictional band too, had the technology been readily available in the early 1990s.

But if Steven – like Bret Easton Ellis – is excellent at creating 'a good impression' of other people, in 'Anesthetize', he adopts the first-person viewpoint; again creating empathy with the central character – the teenage boy – an empathy that's largely missing from the novel.

Alex Lifeson of the rock band, Rush, plays the guitar solo at around four minutes in. Steven told *Prog Archives* that he read a magazine article saying Lifeson was a Porcupine Tree fan, causing Steven to almost fall off his chair, as he'd grown up listening to Rush. Steven got in touch with Lifeson via the article's writer and asked him to play the solo on the album. Steven said, with evident satisfaction – referring also to Robert Fripp (see below): 'It's kind of coming full circle for me now, as the people I grew up listening to are now playing on Porcupine Tree records.' The solo is striking in its use of a slightly Middle-Eastern-flavoured scale: played high on the fretboard, bringing an exotic and other-worldly quality.

Part II: 'The Pills I'm Taking'

Part II has a direct link to *Lunar Park*: in particular, chapter 10, 'The Mall', in which Robby and his disaffected friends are, in the words of the song, '...lost in the mall/Shuffling through stores like zombies'. This image is reminiscent of George A. Romero's zombie movie, *Dawn of the Dead* (1978), which was filmed in Monroeville Mall, Pennsylvania. The film was widely considered as a critique of consumerism, but the song's protagonist is unable to share in the joys of shopping: 'Well what is the point?/What can money buy?'. His mind is filled with 'cod philosophy' due to his excessive Reality TV consumption, which Steven described to Cornelia Wickel of *Guest Musicalypse* as 'ignorant, shallow TV ... I know a lot of people in the world like that, and that they don't really have any kind of aspirations intellectually at all.'

In the novel, the narrator is concerned that his son Robby and his friends are so over-medicated, that their lives are completely devoid of poetry or romance, and that everything they do is automatic – a 'performance', which relates back to the idea of characters doing a good 'impression' of themselves in part one of the song. But there is some degree of poetry here: 'The dust in my soul/Makes me feel the weight in my legs': a memorable, evocative image.

Part II begins with a ferociously frenetic riff on several guitars at once, juddering across multiple time signatures. The following chords bring a more straightforward rock riff, but a ghostly choir, echoes high above, suggesting the central character's blankness and the dust floating in his soul – where there should be youthful passion and energy. The vocals are heavily compressed – almost spectral in tone – mirroring the protagonist's alienation and isolation.

As the vocals enter, the bass line crashes in: thrillingly visceral, like a machine grinding the soul to dust. What's remarkable is the benign, gently smiling, almost wistful expression that bassist Colin Edwin's wears as he plays the song on the live DVD.

Anyone who's spent hours watching late-night TV or streaming services – endlessly scrolling through social media or clickbait articles – will empathize with the strange modern state where it's impossible to switch off the mind (or the TV and smartphone) even though a frustrating boredom prevails: 'I'm totally bored/But I can't switch off.' This may seem like an early 21st-century phenomenon, but T. S. Eliot expressed the feeling of apathy and ennui much earlier, particularly in his poems, 'The Love Song of J. Alfred Prufrock' (1915) and 'The Waste Land' (1922).

The repeated chorus vocal refrain of 'It's all in me, all in you' is a real earworm that would sit well in a pop song; but the grim riff that opened this section viciously cuts the repeated sequence's third cycle short. Although Steven's pop sensibility is well-developed elsewhere (particularly in the Blackfield project) he doesn't allow it to dominate here. There's also an instrumental section, in which the melody is reminiscent of the chorus in Depeche Mode's 'Enjoy the Silence' (1990).

For a few seconds, it feels like there might be respite from the jagged heavy metal onslaught, but then comes an explosive middle eight section, in which all the guitar parts join in, playing in unison – viciously exciting.

Gavin Harrison's drumming is astonishing throughout this section; it's easy to see why he's been voted Drummer of the Year several times *Prog* magazine. He has used this part of the song in his solo drum clinics to demonstrate the combination of power, subtlety, energy and technique across a huge kit. 'The Pills I'm Taking' appeared on Gavin's 2015 solo album *Cheating the Polygraph*. (The album title was taken from track three of *Nil Recurring*: the companion EP to *Fear of a Blank Planet*). The version on Gavin's solo album is very different from 'Anesthetize' as it's arranged for big band by the bass player Laurence Cottle.

Part III: 'Surfer'

Most bands would've ended the song at this point, but Steven takes it into a completely different world.

Pattering synth sounds like drops of welcome rain, punctuate a sampled male-voice choir. In the distance, there's a subtle repeated sample: like the passage in Pink Floyd's 'Dogs' (from *Animals* 1977), where the word 'stone' – from the line 'dragged down by the stone' – echoes into a musical passage that describes the protagonist, drowning. As in 'Dogs', water plays a major part here. But for a while, the scene is calm: 'water so warm that day ... I smiled into the sun.'

John Wesley's gorgeous backing vocals strengthen the moment's beauty. (Wesley also played guitar on the album tour). Interestingly, in the live version on the *Anesthetize* DVD, this section is played slightly slower, giving it a more laid-back feel. In both versions, the vocal parts float across each other, perfectly evoking the 'waves breaking into surf'. Richard Barbieri's subtle keyboard touches – Hammond organ and electric piano – add to the overwhelming feeling of warmth and tranquillity, perhaps matching Part II's drug-induced state of mind.

Steven's vocal in the next verse – on 'the water so warm that day' – is recorded very close, giving it a confessional and intimate quality. But we soon pass from a nostalgic memory to a feeling of aching loss, as the addressee turns his or her back on the protagonist and is then is stolen from him as a dark cloud passes 'across the sun'. This passage feels autobiographical, although not explicitly so; the *Lunar Park* influence is not strong here, and we're far away from the shuffling mall zombies, even though the anaesthesia theme is still present.

When the vocal harmonies return, there's a melancholy quality to 'the water so warm that day' now that we've heard about the break-up. The choir returns, and the song falls into a desolate silence.

'Sentimental' (5:26)

On 4 June 2007, NPR (National Public Radio) in America chose this track as their Song of the Day, which means over 1,000 public US radio stations picked it up. Writer, Cecile Cloutier, reviewed the song under the heading 'Progressive Rock Gets Mordantly Witty'.

The wit arises mainly from the tension between the charmingly calm chorus (particularly the third time with John Wesley's smooth backing vocals) and the lyrics, which describe the 'sullen and bored' kids who are 'stoned in the mall' again. It would be easy to miss the message here, but we're back in the mall with the shuffling zombies and firmly back in Bret Easton Ellis territory. Cecile Cloutier described the murmured vocals as making the words 'sound like wind rattling through dead branches'.

The *Lunar Park* themes are referenced in the verse as well. One of the book's major concerns is the relationship between parents and children: in particular, that between Bret and his son Robby, and also Bret and his own father. In 'Sentimental', the protagonist doesn't want to get old or have children, because once you have your own dependents, 'You can't blame your parents anymore'. This contrasts with the track, 'Normal' (from *Nil Recurring*: this album's companion EP), in which the central character would *like* to get old and 'a little sentimental'. The songs are two sides of the same coin, and they even share the same chorus.

For a fleeting moment, we get a deeper insight into the protagonist's soul in the heart-wrenching line: 'I'm finding it hard to hang from a star.' There's a sense of yearning – a longing for something beyond the almost catatonic state in which he spends his days.

The song opens with Richard Barbieri's slightly syncopated piano chords. Gavin Harrison's delicate but robust drumming matches the mood perfectly, showing that, when required, he can be graceful.

The track's structure and atmosphere are very simple and a good contrast to the previous track's epic length and complexity. Steven has often spoken of the importance of album track sequencing, both with the band and his later solo material (this was one of the reasons he was initially reluctant to put his solo work on streaming services, as they allowed listeners to isolate songs for a playlist, rather than listen to the whole record). Sometimes this means a high-quality song that doesn't fit the sequence is abandoned or released elsewhere: as is the case here when some of the leftover songs appeared on *Nil Recurring*. Speaking in late 2020 about the release of his sixth solo album, *The Future Bites,* Steven said he was concerned about listener attention span and that he was coming back around to the idea of an album (such as the classics originally released on vinyl) being no more than 40 minutes long. So, *The Future Bites* is that length. This, of course, would've meant leaving one or even two tracks off *Fear of a Blank Planet*, which is difficult to contemplate.

The guitar part before the final chorus is reminiscent of the guitar in 'Trains' from *In Absentia*, in which Steven expresses his nostalgia for trains of his childhood. The opening of the next song draws on this nostalgia and longing: 'Out at the train tracks/I dream of escape.'

'Way Out of Here' (Richard Barbieri, Colin Edwin, Gavin Harrison, Steven Wilson) (7:37)

This song perfectly demonstrates two of Steven's favourite and most successful vocal techniques. It begins with one of his most beautiful vocal lines: intimate and delicately poised between speech and melody, creating empathy with the protagonist, who is dreaming of escape. The chorus then changes focus completely, with a full-voiced delivery expressing the main character's desperate need to find a 'way out of here'. Steven uses these vocal production techniques on his voice on his solo albums as well. Compare the verse and chorus of 'Harmony Korine', from *Insurgentes* (2008). The building of multiple track layers gives the choruses a huge sound.

Colin Edwin's bass begins to cut through at around two minutes in. Then the 'mordant wit' that Cecile Cloutier praised in her 'Sentimental' review appears again in the lines referring to forgetting a lover: 'In a thousand years/Or maybe a week.' A mellow guitar passage leads to an aggressive heavy metal riff, perhaps suggesting the contrasting teenage moods of lethargy and anger.

The track ends with Edwin's gorgeous repeating bass line, as synth chords drift into the ether, expressing escape as the song fades out and eventually vanishes – just like the protagonist.

The album liner notes credit 'soundscaping' to King Crimson guitarist Robert Fripp, who supported Porcupine Tree on their 2005 North American Tour. Steven Wilson told *Prog Archives* that Fripp is 'one of the most important musicians, if not the most important musician, in my whole life'.

Steven worked closely with Fripp on remixes of many King Crimson albums. It was a fruitful relationship. Sid Smith described the pair's working relationship in his definitive and comprehensive book, *In the Court of King Crimson*:

> Often Fripp would suggest deletions or significant alterations, which Wilson would then have to resist, in a sense defending the original instrumental decisions: 'I'd say 'No, you can't do that, Robert', which is odd really I suppose, but he would nearly always defer, saying that he trusted my judgement as a fan who would know what other fans would want.'

Joining the band on tour, Fripp played a solo set of pieces using his 'Soundscapes' technique: using digital-delay and looping pedals to create layered soundscapes in real-time. Fripp first used this technique in the early 1970s – before digital technology was available – using two reel-to-reel tape recorders linked together, christening the technique with the delightful name Frippertronics. The resulting ambient drones can be heard on the 1973 album, *No Pussyfooting*: Fripp's collaboration with Brian Eno, who'd been working with tape delay techniques originally developed by the composers Terry Riley and Pauline Oliveros.

The 'Way Out of Here' video is an edited version of Lasse Hoile's projections made for Porcupine Tree's 2007 world tour. Steven's website says the video is 'dedicated to Arielle Daniel: a girl who was killed by a train on 12 November 2005, at the age of seventeen, together with a friend of hers – Heather Bates – who was fourteen years old. Arielle was a big Porcupine Tree fan who founded the band's Myspace Group.

Various online posts state that on 2 June 2007 – when the band played a show in Arielle's hometown of Milwaukee, Wisconsin – members of her family were present, and Steven dedicated her favourite Porcupine Tree song, 'Blackest Eyes' to her memory. They performed 'Way Out of Here' without the video as a mark of respect.

'Sleep Together' (7:28)

On the face of it, this song seems to be about teenage sex. The chorus begins, 'Let's sleep together right now/Relieve the pressure somehow.' We seem to be back in the world of the teenage boy from the opening title track, in which sex is 'kinda fun', but just another way of 'using up a day'. There's also a sense of taking the pressure off a relationship by having sex to get that sometimes difficult issue out of the way.

But there seems to be another meaning, playing on the words 'sleep together': not only is it a euphemism for the sex act, but there's the suggestion that the protagonist and addressee will 'sleep together' in death. There may also be a suggestion of the idea of orgasm being a kind of death, which appears in Shakespeare plays, especially in relation to the star-crossed teenage lovers in *Romeo and Juliet*. The lyric also plays on the idea of orgasm as a release, just as death is a release from life: 'This means out/This is your way out.' The song ends with the words, 'Switch off the future right now/Let's sleep forever' – they will sleep together in death, perhaps as the result of a suicide pact. The request that all evidence of the protagonist be erased, including his clothes, heightens the sense of escape. Steven is unable to resist a subtle dig at the superficial protagonist contemplating his own death – referring to the burning of his designer trainers.

Generally, Steven unconsciously absorbs his musical influences, but as he told Roy Povarchik of *Alternative Zine* in June 2007: 'There is one exception, which is that I wanted the track 'Sleep Together' to sound like Nine Inch Nails, with John Bonham on drums, and produced by Massive Attack!'

The song begins with the sound of synthesized gears grinding into life, above which Steven's sweet falsetto voice floats like that of a choirboy, but with a touch of adult cynicism. In the chorus, his voice gains urgency and is more compressed. Looped backing vocals echo hauntingly in the chorus background.

The synthesized gears continue to grind throughout the song, making it feel like an organic whole. Unusually for a song at this stage of the band's career, there's no epic guitar solo or unison prog metal riffing. Instead, a lovely electric piano solo subtly offsets the continuing synth grinding, a guitar echoing the same musical motif.

The London Session Orchestra greatly enriches the track's soundscape through Dave Stewart and Steven's arrangement. The melodic chromaticism is similar to the repeating string riff in Led Zeppelin's 'Kashmir' from *Physical Graffiti* (1975) and has the same mesmeric effect.

The song ends with Gavin Harrison's surprise solo drum flourish, rounding off the album nicely.

The Incident (2009)

Personnel:
Steven Wilson: vocals, guitars, keyboards
Richard Barbieri: synthesizers, keyboards
Colin Edwin: bass, double bass
Gavin Harrison: drums, percussion
John Wesley: guitars
Recorded at Air Lyndhurst, Monkey Puzzle, No Man's Land, The Artillery, Nightspace, and Red Room Recorders – September 2008 to May 2009.
Producer: Porcupine Tree
Mixer: Steven Wilson
Engineer: Steve Orchard
Release date: September 2009
Chart placings: UK: 23, USA: 25
Grammy nomination: Best Surround Sound Album (2010)
Running time: CD One: 55:08; CD Two: 20:35
Record Label: Roadrunner Records

The Incident is the tenth and final Porcupine Tree album. After its release, there were rumours of a follow-up for a while, and fans still lament the loss of the band, hoping they choose to record or tour again. But the writing was already on the wall by the time *The Incident* came out, due to Steven's first solo album – *Insurgentes* – being released almost a year earlier. But *Insurgentes* still had Porcupine Tree links (photographer Lasse Hoile and drummer Gavin Harrison), and the track 'Harmony Korine' could've sat happily on a Porcupine Tree album.

Though it may not have been obvious at that the time, *The Incident* marked Steven's conscious uncoupling from the band. After its release, he continued working with the Israeli singer, Aviv Geffen, on the third Blackfield album, *Welcome to My DNA*, recorded in 2010 and issued the following year. Simultaneously, Steven worked on his second solo album, *Grace for Drowning* (2011), and his collaboration with Opeth's Mikael Åkerfeldt was also in progress, leading to the 2012 album *Storm Corrosion*.

As Porcupine Tree's main creative force, Steven respected the other members' musical interests. In an interview with *FaceCulture* on YouTube in August 2009 he said that what made Porcupine Tree special was the tiny four-circle crossover like a Venn diagram, where the four members met in the middle. But existing in such a small musical space can become claustrophobic. Steven was happy to be limited within the band, as it gave their work focus; but eventually, he found working on his solo material liberating. He told Anil Prasad in an interview for *Innerviews.org* in spring 2010: 'If I want to fuse a beautiful orchestral passage with a complete wall of noise within a pop song with trip hop elements – all in the space of eight minutes – I can. And that's what I did with *Insurgentes*. (The song was 'Salvaging').

At the point when he'd written thirty minutes of music for *The Incident*, but no lyrics, he was looking for a theme. Suddenly, a strange, gruesomely poetic image struck him: he was driving home from the studio. The motorway traffic suddenly narrowed to one lane, slowing down to a traffic jam. He realised there'd been an accident, seeing a sign that said 'Slow Down – Police Incident'. It struck him that the word 'incident' was a very detached, impersonal way of labelling a brutally traumatic personal tragedy: in this case, a car crash which was probably fatal.

His account of the event is somewhat unclear. On his website, he said he 'had the sensation that the spirit of someone that had died in the accident, entered into my car and was sitting next to me'. In the *FaceCulture* interview, he said he could see dead people in his rear-view mirror. What is clear is that the horrific crash caused a feeling in him that – as he told Lilen Pautasso of *Reverb Online* in August 2009 – was 'very dark and ghostly and a little bit creepy'. He told *FaceCulture* the experience was like something out of *The Twilight Zone*, thus creating a degree of detachment, but he also accepted that this 'incident' had revealed to him something about human nature. Steven said we have to use neutral language in describing horrific events. The emergency services must look such horrors in the eye, but for the rest of us, the word 'incident' sanitises reality, making it bearable, as he said on his website: 'The irony of such a cold expression for such seismic events, appealed to me.' He began to notice that in news broadcasts, the word 'incident' was often used to describe catastrophic human tragedy. A further irony is that part of human nature is to *want* to look at the car crash – we can't divert our eyes – which is why the motorway traffic had stopped on that night. Although for reasons of taste and decency, parts of the media choose not to show us life's brutal realities, there's an opposite, expressed in the phrase: 'If it bleeds, it leads' – in other words, horrific incidents make it onto the front page.

Steven started collecting the human stories behind similar incidents reported in the media so dispassionately, fictionalising the backgrounds and some details, so they became stories, rather than news reports. He also added a degree of emotional truth to incidents that had 'a certain sickness at the core': a process he found disturbing as both a listener and a writer.

He wrote the songs in the first-person, as miniature human dramas, like short films: a technique he'd adopted so well in songs like 'Heartattack in a Layby' on *In Absentia*. But he also began exploring his own life incidents, writing some of his most autobiographical songs ever. He told Lilen Pautasso he found himself drawn to the 'darker, more twisted sides of life' and wanted to explore the parallels and contrasts between his own life and the incidents he was writing about.

By his own admission, Steven's life has been relatively comfortable and free of trauma, so why constantly turn to darker subjects? He may have experienced a catharsis writing about the human psyche's darker side. In 2005, he told Anil Prasad of *Innerviews.org*:

In order to write music, I have to be depressed. I was never really aware of this until the last couple of years. I usually create music when I'm in a negative state of mind. It is quite a painful process. I love recording, touring and promoting the records, but the art of writing music is very much a cathartic and painful one for me. People ask me to reconcile my personality – which is not melancholic or dark – with the music that very much represents those things. My explanation is that the music is where that side of me goes. The music is an exorcism of those elements within.

'The Incident' is a long 14-song sequence, beginning with 'Occam's Razor' and ending with 'I Drive the Hearse'. An additional four songs are not part of the song cycle. Steven tried to write a continuous and complete song cycle in the past with *The Sky Moves Sideways* (1995) but eventually gave up and wrote shorter songs instead. *The Incident* marked the first time he felt he was able to write 'a long-form musical novel, having focused on short stories before'. As he told Lilen Pautasso he wanted to create a 'cinematic sweep' and to continue the movie analogy, his aim was to produce a series of scenes that rather than having a simple Hollywood blockbuster-style narrative structure, delivered the surreal juxtapositions of a European art film. Musically, it was a complete sequence; lyrically, the concept was much looser than the previous album, *Fear of a Blank Planet*.

For the album cover, Steven asked his long-term collaborator, Lasse Hoile, to create an image showing the way the media represents 'incidents' involving celebrities: Steven described an image depicting a celebrity leaving a courthouse, putting a hand in front of his face to avoid paparazzi, like the famous Mick Jagger picture: Jagger handcuffed to art dealer Robert Fraser following their 1967 court appearance on drug charges, of which they were both convicted. They are sitting in a vehicle, wearing suits, and both have a protective hand covering their faces.

All music and lyrics by Steven Wilson, except where marked.

Cd One 'The Incident: Parts I – Xiv'
I: 'Occam's Razor' (1:55)
This instrumental track begins with a real statement of intent: three groups of three guitar power chords of the sort used in heavy rock and heavy metal. Steven wanted to start the song sequence with an almost primaeval big bang. He told Anil Prasad that the work of American composer, John Adams, influenced him – specifically Adams' piece 'Harmonielehre' (1985), which starts with what Tom Service in *The Guardian* in March 2014, called a 'battering ram' of no fewer than 39 repeated E minor chords. Adams said he wanted to hark back to conventional tonal harmony, which many orchestral composers had abandoned in the early 20th century.

The opening distorted chords immediately give the album a sense of unease and ambiguity; the following tentative acoustic guitar chords intensifying the unsettling feeling. After the power chords return, the track dissolves into anxious noise before gently taking up the next track's theme. What had begun as a powerful statement using conventional heavy rock chords has already entered a much darker world.

II: 'The Blind House' (5:47)

We are now plunged into the darkness of the album's first 'incident', which is based on the story of a police raid on the Yearning for Zion ranch in Texas: home of cult leader Warren Jeffs – the polygamist leader of the Fundamentalist Church of Jesus Christ of Latter-Day Saints – currently serving life-plus-twenty-years for sex with minors who he'd married. In the 2008 raid, 400 children were rescued and brought into the custody of the State of Texas, and 133 women left the compound of their own volition. It was a newspaper photograph of the police marching one of the girls from the compound, that inspired the song. As Steven told *FaceCulture*, she was looking directly at the camera: 'Her eyes just spoke so much to me.'

The CD booklet includes Lasse Hoile's photographs of women in ankle-length dresses (the cult uniform), including one where a woman puts her hand up to block the camera: mirroring the front cover image.

The song starts with a heavy, dystopian, distorted metal riff, including a distinctive semitone drop from a D# power chord to a D. Guitars are tuned down to drop-D for much of the album.

In some ways, it's a classic late-era Porcupine Tree song; immediately after the heavy riff is an almost psychedelic section. The opening words – delivered as sweet and insouciant – are from the imaginary cult leader's viewpoint (Jeffs is never named), intertwined with his captives' thoughts, suggesting they have a symbiotic relationship, or even that there may be an element of Stockholm Syndrome at play. Richard Barbieri's spangly synth part strengthens the ambiguity. Later the song enters an almost electronic section; the three music genres combining.

But the lines 'Free love/Bring love to all my sisters' are free of ambiguity, interspersed with the simplest of two-chord metal riffs. This is not an offer of 1960s hippie-type freedom, nor of sexual equality. Instead, it is made entirely on the cult leader's terms. Calling the women and girls 'my sisters', is hardly an expression of solidarity but rather a sinister confirmation of patriarchy.

At around four minutes in, the track seemingly reaches its natural end, entering a surreal dreamscape of industrial electronic percussion, sounding slightly sour and metallic, like someone hitting a metal bucket with a stick. It's as if we're experiencing the ranch from the viewpoint of the blind house itself – breathing out as the free love is offered to the 'sisters who live there'.

The intro's heavy riff returns one final time, doubled with thirds above, adding menace, only to be suddenly cut off.

III: 'Great Expectations' (1:26)

The title comes from Charles Dickens' 1861 novel, in which the orphaned Pip's expectation that receiving wealth from a mysterious benefactor will improve his life proves to be more complex than he'd hoped. The expectation also relates to Pip's childhood longing for the remote and frigid figure of Estella.

The song also touches on the loss of childhood's hopes and friendship. The opening image of a summer day expresses childhood innocence, reinforced through melodious acoustic guitars and the gentle, intimate opening lines' delivery. But that innocence is soon shattered: to the accompaniment of a bitter, brittle rising guitar line and turbulent, disquieting drums, we discover that Steven has lost touch with his placid-eyed childhood friend, and has even forgotten his name. His friend's fate is unclear, but he was locked up: either in prison, a mental institution, or perhaps both.

In less than 90 seconds, the song perfectly encapsulates a major album theme: how lives can change in unexpected ways. The boy is oblivious to what is to come, and the contrast with Steven's own life – and the very different path he took – is delicately implied rather than overtly stated.

IV: 'Kneel and Disconnect' (2:03)
A gentle, almost psychedelic song with beautiful harmonies and a lovely piano motif – minus drums or percussion of any sort.

Steven described the track as referring to the time when he decided to give up his lucrative computer industry job to become a professional musician: a major life 'incident' which he described in a YouTube interview for Roadrunner Records in November 2009 as a 'landmark moment'.

The idea of kneeling and disconnecting suggests that his previous job involved being subservient to his employer and a conventional career while disconnecting his mind from the work in order to escape.

V: 'Drawing the Line' (4:43)
Richard Barbieri's opening keyboards are delightful, as are Gavin Harrison's loose-limbed and beautifully-recorded drums. Steven's singing in the verse, is as sweet as ever, echoed by Barbieri's ghostly, ethereal, but almost human-sounding synth line.

In October 2009, Chris Conaton said on the *PopMatters* website that the 'chorus becomes the album's most effective combination of melody and urgency'. It's certainly an earworm, but the vocal delivery is rather strained. Is Steven sounding tired and frustrated about the band as he sees it coming to a natural end? Or is that just hindsight? Whichever view you take, the vocals on the version from the live album, *Octane Twisted*, are delivered with much more passion and conviction.

VI: 'The Incident' (5:20)
If you're listening to the album while you read this, you should turn this track up loud and simply revel in the visceral joy of the evocative soundscaping.

The track begins with grinding, writhing electronics: darkly evocative of the previous album's 'Sleep Together'. Then an eerie whispering voice repeats an unintelligible mantra.

The ominously muttered opening lyric lines place us instantly – and with poetic economy – at the heart of the 'incident' that gave the album its title: 'At junction 8, the traffic starts to slow/Artilleries of braking lights and bluish glow.' This works so well because it's so precise. It's an interesting contrast to the opening image of the song 'Permanating' (from Steven's 2017 solo album, *To the Bone*): 'Somewhere on the highway/With a luminous moon' – another road image, but in this case, poetic in its deliberately-generic vagueness.

The song's theme is disturbing: 'When a car crash gets you off, you've lost your grip.' A recognised psychiatric disorder exists called symphorophilia: the sexual arousal experienced from staging and watching car crashes. This unusual fetish is the subject of J. G. Ballard's 1973 novel, *Crash*, in which the central character – Dr. Robert Vaughan – stages car crashes for his own sexual gratification. Reviewers at the time were horrified. Film critic Roger Ebert, writing on his website in March 1997 about David Cronenberg's 1996 film adaptation, put it simply: 'Of course there is no connection between eroticism and automobile accidents.' That should be the final word on the matter, but the book is strangely compelling. Reading it is like watching a car crash: you feel guilty about doing so but can't quite tear yourself away.

VII: 'Your Unpleasant Family' (1:48)

It's hard to know what to make of this track. Part of the difficulty is the immediate follow-on from 'The Incident', at the same tempo; but there's something uneasy about the transition. And it's difficult to know how to take the lyrics: 'Your unpleasant family/Smashed up my car' must be one of the strangest song openings ever. It links to the tragic car accident of the previous song – 'I crawled out of the wreckage on my knees' – but the link is unconvincing, sung in such gorgeous, sensual harmonies.

Unusually for Porcupine Tree, the track's tone is difficult to gauge. Presumably, the tone is sarcastic. This certainly seems to apply to smashing up the car being 'perfectly uncalled for': a polite, understated English phrase that seems odd in this context.

In a revealing interview with Anil Prasad of *Innerviews.org* in 2010, Steven explained the track's unusual jangly guitar sound. Paul Reed Smith (from PRS Guitars) offered to make Steven a baritone guitar. He told Anil he'd always admired Swedish band, Meshuggah's guitar sound: where they took a baritone guitar, tuned the lower strings even lower, and taped up the top strings. Steven asked PRS to make him a guitar with an additional piezo pickup, which would amplify the string sounds themselves (rather than turn the string vibrations into electrical impulses, which is what most electric guitar pick-ups do). Piezo pickups are normally used on acoustic guitars that have nylon strings, which a magnetic pick-up wouldn't adequately amplify. In this case, Steven wanted to hear the glitchy string sounds. He even told Anil: 'This particular guitar informs a lot of the heavier stuff on the album.' The baritone's longer neck means the strings are longer and can be tuned lower than a conventional guitar. The bottom string – depending on the tuning method – is usually a B or an A: several notes lower than a conventional guitar's bottom E.

VIII: 'The Yellow Windows of the Evening Train' (2:00)

Another train song, but this time an instrumental. Like its more famous sibling, 'Trains', from *In Absentia*, it has a nostalgic feel. The main instrument sounds like a Mellotron: instantly recognisable, giving a certain nostalgic feel. Steven also added the sound of a crackling vinyl record. As he told Anil Prasad: 'One of the great ironies of the way I make albums, is that I record completely digitally, yet people say my records sound like vintage '70s records.'

The track acts as a little nostalgic interlude: a taster for the next track.

IX 'Time Flies' (11:40)

On the Roadrunner Records YouTube channel in August 2009, Steven described this as an autobiographical song: not about a specific 'incident', but something that changed his life forever – one of five or six landmark life moments after which nothing would be the same again: '...something protracted, like a relationship that didn't go very well, or something instantaneous like a car accident, something that happens in a split second, a moment of concentration lost, and your life changes or potentially ends.'

The track starts at the beginning of Steven's life: 'I was born in '67/The year of *Sgt. Pepper* and *Are You Experienced*'. 1967 was also the year in which Pink Floyd released their debut album *The Piper at the Gates of Dawn*. Steven has acknowledged his debt to Pink Floyd, citing his father playing *Dark Side of the Moon* (1973) when Steven was eight years old, as one of his earliest and most important musical influences; his website biography describes this album and Donna Summer's *Love To Love You Baby* (1975) as 'pivotal in the development of his musical direction'.

'Time Flies' owes an obvious debt to another Pink Floyd album, *Animals* (1977): in particular, 'Dogs', which at seventeen minutes long, is a good five minutes longer than 'Time Flies'. The most obvious reference points are the intro's driving and mesmeric acoustic guitar rhythm and the instrumental break at around three minutes in.

'Time Flies' is a fan favourite, and Steven has never hidden Pink Floyd's influence on his work: thrillingly expressed here in one of Porcupine Tree's best songs. And it seems appropriate that such an autobiographical song should pay homage to one of Steven's earliest musical influences. But more recently, he's has distanced himself from this. On Tim Burgess' Twitter Listening Party in July 2020, he said, 'They frequently influence my songs, but those songs have tended to become my least favourites ... as I prefer to create my own musical world.'

There are more subtle Pink Floyd echoes. Both 'Time Flies' and 'Dogs' use the phrase 'after a while' to describe the passage of time: 'But after a while, you realise time flies' ('Time Flies'); and 'after a while, you can work on points for style' ('Dogs'). But the way the songs deal with the time concept contrasts starkly. Steven's song is relatively nostalgic and sentimental, particularly in the early section; whereas the Pink Floyd song is brutal in its assessment of the protagonist and his relationship with time: eventually, it becomes too late for him to lose the weight he used to need to throw around, and he ends up a lonely, sad old man, dying of cancer.

'Time Flies' was the album's only single, released – ironically – in a shortened five-and-a-half-minute version. This is perfectly understandable, but also a great pity, as the instrumental, starting at around four minutes into the album version, is one of the band's best such passages. Steven takes us into a dreamlike state, where gentle acoustic guitar arpeggios contrast first with a higher guitar melody played through multiple effects, then with a lower melody moving at a more stately pace, drenched in reverb and delay. This melody's unexpected semitone intervals touch the soul deeply, though it's hard to explain exactly why. Then, an incredibly urgent burst of drums suddenly disrupts the elegant calm while guitars squall high above.

Steven is an expert at layering textures that build to a portentous climax. (Perhaps the only other band who can build an atmosphere in this way is King Crimson). He achieves a similar effect at the end of 'Abandoner' (from his first solo album *Insurgentes*), which he was working on around the same time as *The Incident*. On that track, he combines the lowest piano notes with layered baritone guitars, producing a sound that seems to come from a primaeval place, and which speaks to the deepest human urges.

Lasse Hoile's video begins with the idyll of Steven's childhood – the countryside and scenes from a 'suburban heaven' – including, of course, the obligatory railway arches. The video – like the song – shows various stages in Steven's early relationships, including a scene where two young women appear to fight over him. Faces in the video are deliberately blurred, as if to protect anonymity, although, like Steven, the young man does wear glasses. The lyric images, too, are mostly deliberately elusive, although they clearly mean a lot to Steven.

But the song does turn darker, with a reference to the young woman's family being 'deranged': the same 'unpleasant family' who smashed up his car?

The song ends with a yearning, poetic image of a teenage girl and the coat she wore on a trip to Alton Towers theme park: the way Steven will always remember her – capturing a tender moment in the relationship.

X: 'Degree Zero of Liberty' (1:45)

The song begins with the opening chords from 'Occam's Razor', reinforcing the sense of song cycle: making the musical theme a character in the unfolding drama.

The track feels like a musical punctuation mark, allowing us to catch our breath. It features beautifully recorded, contemplative guitar – distorted but mellow – very similar to the sound and style of Opeth guitarist Mikael

Åkerfeldt. This isn't surprising considering Steven's work as Opeth producer, and the fact that at the time, he and Mikael Åkerfeldt were both playing PRS guitars: which combine lyrical sweetness with fearsome growls – rather like Mikael's own singing.

XI: 'Octane Twisted' (Steven Wilson, Colin Edwin, Gavin Harrison, Richard Barbieri) (5:03)

According to Steven's website, this song refers to 'a body found floating in a river by some people on a fishing trip': another 'incident', described here in appropriately dispassionate language, as if in a news report.

The whole band wrote the piece, though Steven wrote the lyrics. It's a microcosm of all that is great about Porcupine Tree. It also illustrates how far away from conventional pop structures some of their songs can be. Rather than intro/verses/choruses/middle eight/verses/choruses/fade, this song has five sections, a couple of which are repeated.

It begins with electric and acoustic guitars in a contemplative mood. At one minute in, a melodic section with lush vocal harmonies ruminates on the 'blood spilling out of the reeds'. At 1:40, there's a sudden heavy riff with gothic voice samples, as if expressing the true horror of finding the body. At 2:00, is a funky section with syncopated guitar chords and a spacey rising keyboard motif. At 2:50, the heavy riff returns, and at 3.10, the funky guitar section returns with a looping theme. At 4:00, the final section begins with psychedelic keyboards: a showcase for Richard Barbieri's subtle colourings and Gavin Harrison's virtuoso drumming.

The song lends its name to the live album released in November 2012.

XII: 'The Séance' (2:39)

This track uses the same chord sequence from the previous song's intro: a sequence also used in 'The Blind House.' 'The Séance' conjures up an image of the body found in the previous song, as evidenced by the repetition of the line: 'blood spilling out of the reeds'. This is made more explicit through Lasse Hoile's photographs taken for the album. For the track, 'Octane Twisted', the CD booklet shows what appears to be a white dress stained with blood; and for 'The Séance', a fairly generic circle of hands. Many more of Lasse's photos for the album can be found in his book, *Muzak The Visual Art of Porcupine Tree*, in which the story of 'Octane Twisted' and 'The Séance' is much clearer: a man with a knife chases a young woman in a white dress and murders her.

The song is a gentle, wistful ballad, taking us into an almost dreamlike state, as a disembodied hand appears to those attending the séance. (For those seeking a true sense of the supernatural in Steven's music, it's worth investigating his 2013 solo album *The Raven That Refused to Sing*: in particular, the title track, which poignantly explores an old man's relationship with his long-dead sister).

XIII: 'Circle of Manias' (Steven Wilson, Colin Edwin, Gavin Harrison, Richard Barbieri) (2:18)

As Steven told Anil Prasad in 2010, this track uses the baritone guitar (see 'Your Unpleasant Family' above) tuned down very low. Coming after a gentle acoustic ballad, it's amazingly visceral: probably the heaviest Porcupine Tree riff of all. Steven said it comes from him 'loving the sound of extreme metal records, but not loving the records themselves that much'.

The song seems to be influenced by Swedish extreme metal band, Meshuggah, whose records the Porcupine Tree members listened to on tour before they recorded *In Absentia*. The main riff is brutal, circling around itself awkwardly in a manic 9/8 time, perhaps evoking the song title. The additional ninth quaver (or 8th note) in each bar (usually in a rock song, there are eight rather than nine) creates an uneasy limping rhythm. At just over one minute in, there's an incredibly effective moment when the drums briefly drop out, and the riff continues to grind menacingly. The track slightly loses its power towards the end when the swift chord changes detract from the main riff, but even so, it remains a very powerful song.

XIV: 'I Drive The Hearse' (6:41)

This is one of Steven's most difficult and troubling songs: partly due to the subject matter, but also because of the metaphorically dense lyrics, making interpretation difficult. On one level, it's a tuneful ballad, but the words tell a different story. It's also one of Steven Wilson's finest vocal performances with Porcupine Tree. What follows is an attempt to interpret the song, but its beauty and power come partly from the fact that it's open to interpretation.

The song is about frustration with oneself; maybe even a degree of self-hatred. It appears to be a kind of a meditation on how we do things that are bad for us or how we don't always act in the way we know we should or even want to. This could be one interpretation of *driving one's own hearse*. The title could also relate to depression and even death: 'When I'm lost I dig the dirt/ When I fall I drive the hearse.' The reference to digging the dirt – in the context of driving the hearse – could refer to the protagonist metaphorically digging his own grave, rather than the phrase's more usual meaning: discovering and revealing something damaging about another person.

More generally, the song seems to be about an unhealthy relationship, where communication has broken down, and self-destructive behaviour patterns are rife. Even the simplest lines are ambiguous, such as '...silence is another way/ Of saying what I wanna say'. This could mean the protagonist is frustrated that he's unable to say what he needs to say; or it could mean he's giving someone the silent treatment.

But there is hope at one point: 'Given time I fix the roof': a metaphor for him coming around to making improvements in his life and relationships. But the next line brutally dashes any hope: 'Given cash, I speak the truth,' showing us he has a very cynical impression of himself.

The protagonist is also unclear about who's at fault for the apparent relationship breakdown. Sometimes he seems to blame the other person: 'You were always my mistake'; other times he puts this burden on himself: 'When she cries I take the blame.' He tries to justify his behaviour to the other person, but also perhaps to himself.

CD TWO
'Flicker' (3:42)

This is the first of four freestanding songs – not part of the song cycle – that made up the second CD of the original release. When the album was released as a single CD, a gap of about 40 seconds was left after the song cycle to make it clear it had ended.

When directing his 1962 play, *The Lovers*, playwright Harold Pinter is supposed to have said, 'We're not quite sure of the author's intention here', even though he was the author. Similarly, in the Roadrunner Records YouTube interview in 2009, Steven Wilson said about this song, that he had 'no idea what it is about'. Perhaps he was being disingenuous, but Steven said it was an example of automatic writing: as a surrealism fan, he just put the words together and determined their meaning later. This is similar to David Bowie's cut-up technique, used to randomly form lyrics. He originally used pieces of paper but later developed computer software called the Verbasizer. Novelist, William Burroughs pioneered the technique: an idea taken from the early-20th-century Dadaist movement, which fed into the surrealist movement.

Steven called this song, an example of 'surrealist action art'. This relates to his love of the surreal in art, such as the films of Luis Buñuel and David Lynch, with their nonlinear narratives. On a wider level, Steven applies this principal to his songwriting, using unconventional song structures and different styles and genres within the same song. His refusal to stick to one genre has sometimes caused consternation among fans, and has probably made marketing his music more difficult (The tag 'progressive' is not always adequate). Steven has always had a restless, enquiring intelligence and hates being pigeonholed. In 2005, Anil Prasad of *Innerviews.org* asked what progression there was from *In Absentia* to *Deadwing*, Steven's reply was illuminating:

I'm always relying on the fact that there will be development between records ... It surprises me when other bands don't change from album to album. It is like, 'Has nothing happened to you? Have you had no new experiences?'. So, I know in my head that the new album is a progression.

The fact that the lyrics don't really fit the rhythmic meter (to use a term from poetic theory, they fail to *scan* properly), does perhaps suggest the words did appear unfiltered from Steven's consciousness, remaining unedited.

'Bonnie the Cat' (Steven Wilson, Colin Edwin, Gavin Harrison, Richard Barbieri) (5:45)

Many songs (and other works of art) begin with a working title: most famously Paul McCartney's 'Yesterday', which he called 'Scrambled Eggs' in an early version. It's an easy way of labelling a work in progress. It can also be a way of hiding a project's real identity. Steven Spielberg's 1982 movie *E.T. the Extra-Terrestrial,* was filmed under the title *A Boy's Life* (although an original shooting script for sale online in 2020 was clearly marked Extra-Terrestrial Productions, Inc. in bold type on the front page).

'Bonnie the Cat' was actually the song's working name, taken from the studio cat. Steven liked it so much, he kept the title.

It begins with serene synthesizer chords, like those beginning the Tangerine Dream album, *Phaedra* (1973), which Steven would later remaster. But the calm doesn't last long. Fierce drumming and an agitated and unsettling bass, underpin angry and aggressive spoken verse lyrics. Steven described the song as 'quite twisted', and it has its own sinister power. He said it was about a relationship that did not end well. The lyrics are vitriolic: lines like 'I hold your birth control to ransom/The cells divide and grow inside you', are chilling.

In the Roadrunner interview, Steven said the person he'd broken up with ruined his life and that the song describes the angry stage after a break-up. 'Remember Me Lover' (see below) describes the bitterness that follows.

The chorus vocals are rather strained; as with some of the album's other songs, the live vocals on the live album, *Octane Twisted*, are better. Perhaps Steven wanted to express extreme passion in songs, often keeping the original demo vocal takes, as they were closer to the original sentiment. But would it be too much to detect a certain weariness in his voice, partly because of his growing desire to move on to his solo projects? This theory could hold water, considering that the song feels a bit too long and a little unfinished.

'Black Dahlia' (Stephen Wilson, Richard Barbieri) (3:40)

In the Roadrunner interview, Steven said that the Black Dahlia – real name Elizabeth Short – was an aspiring Hollywood actress whose body was found 'perfectly severed'. The unsolved murder occurred in 1947, and according to an article in the *Los Angeles Times* on 25 March 1996, over 500 people confessed to the murder, even though some weren't even been born when the crime occurred. The case inspired James Ellroy's 1987 novel, *The Black Dahlia*, which became a 2006 Brian De Palma film starring Scarlett Johansson. Steven said this was a 'fascinating story' ... but 'the song has nothing to do with it!'

The title did inspire the mood, to the extent that it's a melancholy study in ambition, the pressure to achieve, and failure to reach one's potential. But maybe it would've been better if Steven had written about the Black Dahlia instead, in one of his dark mini-epics, rather than the fairly bland song it became. Even the opening keyboard motif – a simple repeated 5th from A to E

– sounds a little half-hearted. Strangely, parts of the melody are a precursor to his solo track, 'Song Of Unborn', from *To the Bone* (2017).

'Remember Me Lover' (7:28)

After the anger of 'Bonnie the Cat', this song describes the next post-break-up stage, after the bitterness. Again, the lyrics are deeply unpleasant: 'I hated you/I wish you'd learn to keep your mouth shut.' In the Roadrunner interview Steven said the song is about a break-up with a woman who ditched him, leaving a 'very deep scar'. He said that he's written many songs about her, and she 'casts a shadow' across the rest of his life. This should've created a powerful song; post-break-up bitterness is good subject matter; see Peter Hammill's caustic take on the subject: 'Betrayed' from *Over* (1977).

The problem is, 'Remember Me Lover' is not very interesting: the band sound as if on autopilot in the early parts, recycling old ideas; and the killer riff that should come in near the end, is weak.

The song ends suddenly when the riff stops partway through; we hear a little reverb, and then the band are gone.

Compilation Albums, EPs, Bonus Tracks and Singles

Note: only tracks not reviewed elsewhere are mentioned in detail here. All music and lyrics by Steven Wilson, except where marked.

Yellow Hedgerow Dreamscape (1994)

Personnel:

Steven Wilson: all instruments and vocals, except:

Malcolm Stocks: guitar on 'Landscare' and 'Wastecoat'; voice and drum programming on 'Towel'; guitar and voice on 'An Empty Box'; MC on 'Yellow Hedgerow Dreamscape'

Simon Vockings: synthesiser on 'Landscare'; organ on 'Prayer'

Seamus Teale: organ and guitar on 'Split Image'

Alex Slater: appears as 'alex slater' on 'Track Eleven'

Howard Jones: drums on 'Execution of the Will of the Marquis de Sade'

Record label: Magic Gnome/Headphone Dust

Release date: January 1994

Current release: Unavailable to buy new, or to stream

This album collects the material from two early cassette tapes – *Tarquin's Seaweed Farm* (1989) and *The Nostalgia Factory* (1990) – that Steven Wilson left off of the first official album: *On the Sunday of Life* (1992). The original CD included a cover version of Prince's 'The Cross', but in the 2013 reissue sleeve notes, Steven said he couldn't bring himself to include it. He modestly says of the whole album: 'Please lower your expectations for these very early experiments – despite being cleaned up as much as possible, this is still far from high fidelity sound, and a lot of the music barely rises above the definition of messing about.'

This is essentially a solo album, compiled from material recorded in Steven's home studio between 1984 and 1991. But he did involve a few other people, notably his friend, Malcolm Stocks, for whose 'ears and amusement', much of the music was written. The tracks 'Mute', 'Yellow Hedgerow Dreamscape' and 'An Empty Box', include spoken-word elements; 'Track 11', 'Radioactive Toy' and 'Out' include vocals. The remaining tracks are instrumentals.

'Mute' (8:05)

A mellow instrumental, which adds a confident, funky guitar riff and a gentle guitar solo. At around four minutes in, there's a sudden strange fade, and a slowed-down voice introduces a dystopian vision of the future: 'The mute lie choking in the green fields of England ... burning in a hand-me-down Hiroshima.' The music fades up again, with some lovely fretless bass and another extended guitar solo.

'Landscare' (2:58)
Segued from the previous track, the dystopian vision continues, with a creepy, unintelligible slowed-down voice and horror film synth atmospherics.

'Prayer' (1:38)
Also segued from the previous track, with heavy-echoed flute sounds. The track gives some hope after the horrors of the previous songs.

'Daughters In Excess' (6:34)
This song appears to have been heavily influenced by the wailing guitar parts on 'A Saucerful of Secrets', and the opening riff of 'Set the Controls for the Heart of the Sun', from Pink Floyd's live album, *Ummagumma* (1969); an album with which Steven said he had an 'unnatural obsession, as he told Jess Thompson of *Discogs* in 2017.

'Delightful Suicide' (1:04)
A traditional Indian classical music instrument combines with distorted guitars.

'Split Image' (1:53)
A soundscape of stormy synths with slow organ chords.

'No Reason To Live, No Reason To Die' (11:07)
If this were a full band track, it could be described as a spacey, extended guitar and keyboard jam. It even speeds up as it goes along, as live jams can do as the excitement builds. A live audience is even dubbed on at the climax – at around eight and half minutes in – before the mood changes, the programmed drums drop out, and keyboards dominate for the remainder.

'Wastecoat' (1:11)
An experimental track, sounding like slowed-down and sped-up guitars.

'Towel' (3:37)
A jazzy song with extensive percussion, fretless bass and electric piano, throughout which a long guitar solo threads its way.

'Execution Of The Will Of The Marquis De Sade' (5:07)
The only track to benefit from real drums: played by Howard Jones. As well as disturbing vocal samples, it includes a rather incongruous sample of the song 'Hokey Cokey': an audience participation dance (known as 'Hokey Pokey' in North America).

'Track Eleven' (3:00)

A jolly, vaguely psychedelic track, in the spirit of 'Linton Samuel Dawson' from *On the Sunday of Life*.

'An Empty Box' (3:12)

This begins with a witty spoken exchange about the possible release of 'a box of unreleased demos ... the empty box would be as far as we would get', which leads to laughter that's suddenly interrupted by a spacey, Floydian jam, with fretless bass morphing into psychedelic soundscaping.

'Out' (8.53)

This track from the *Love Death & Mussolini* cassette (1990) replaced 'The Cross' on later versions of the album. Steven described it as a 'Hawkwind pastiche'. The opening lyrics – 'Floating on the winds of time/Space gives way inside my mind' – could've easily come from one of Hawkwind's space rock epics.

'Music for the Head' (1:23)

A short, atmospheric instrumental with no drums, reminiscent of early Tangerine Dream.

Staircase Infinities (1994)

Personnel:
Produced, performed and mixed by: Steven Wilson, February 1992 to May 1993
Recorded at No Man's Land
Release date: 1994, and May 2005 as the second CD of the *Up the Downstair* expanded edition
Chart placings: Did not chart
Running time: 29:44
Record label: Lazy Eye Records (Holland)
Current version: Streaming services

Staircase Infinities was released as an EP in the Netherlands in 1994. On the Porcupine Tree site, Steven said the record, '...was originally put together after we received an offer from Lazy Eye Records in Holland to do a limited edition 10" vinyl EP. I used three leftovers from the abandoned double album of *Up the Downstair* on Side One and recorded two tracks, especially for Side Two, including a new version of a track dating from the cassette years: 'Yellow Hedgerow Dreamscape'.'

The EP is the final release from the early Porcupine Tree days when the band was a Steven Wilson solo project.

At the time of writing, the record is no longer available to buy, except as part of the thirteen-CD box set *Porcupine Tree: The Delerium Years 1991-1997* (Transmission Recordings 2020). It is, however, available on streaming services.

'Cloud Zero' (4:39)

This instrumental begins with synths sounding like early Tangerine Dream before the track morphs into a mixture of dance rhythms and blues guitar riffs, interspersed with more ambient moments. A lively and invigorating opening.

'The Joke's on You' (Steven Wilson, Alan Duffy) (4:05)

This track marks the end of an era: it's the last released Porcupine Tree song with lyrics by Alan Duffy. For the rest of the band's career, Steven wrote all the lyrics. By Duffy's surreal standards, the lyrics are fairly toned down, although the opening verse remains in the realm of fantasy and psychedelia: 'Riding on a unicorn/ Stranded in my mind/Electric raven met me there/To see what we could find.'

After that, the lyrics become much more straightforward, referring to a 'dark star's endless journey' and strange, incredible days.

Musically, the song is also fairly simple, beginning with strummed acoustic guitars, building to an epic chorus, before heading into an ambient section with lovely ambiguous soundscapes and floating chords. If there's one criticism, it's that Steven's voice sounds a little strained in the higher parts of the chorus.

'Navigator' (4:51)

This instrumental is a spacey, psychedelic guitar jam. But the percussion programming sounds slightly dull and uninspired: it lets the track down.

'Rainy Taxi' (6:44)

This instrumental takes its title from Spanish surrealist artist Salvador Dalí's 1938 art installation at Paris' Galerie Beaux-Arts. It consists of two mannequins sitting in a real taxi. The male driver has a shark's head, and the female back seat passenger has live snails crawling across her body, and she's surrounded by lettuce and chicory. Water pipes provide artificial rainfall inside the vehicle.

This ambient track beautifully expresses the atmosphere inside the 'rainy taxi', with dark, brooding organ chords and splashing cymbals that suggest the rain. The distorted spoken words appear to describe the rainy taxi exhibit. Organ accompanies gently-strummed acoustic guitars and a simple bass part. The organ chords give an anthemic feel: the highlight of the EP, reminiscent of the kosmische musik of German bands like Ash Ra Tempel.

'Yellow Hedgerow Dreamscape' (9:24)

Another fine instrumental which is a precursor of a much later song, 'Salvaging', from Steven's first solo album *Insurgentes* (2008).

The first section could be a thriller soundtrack, with its chromatic synth lines and repetitive bass part. At around four minutes, an extended Floydian guitar solo begins as the track gradually speeds up, reminding us that, even in the early days, Steven was an accomplished player. The track gets faster and faster, to the extent that it feels it might eventually explode, until the instruments drop out, leaving an ambient section that could've come from a science fiction film soundtrack: like *Blade Runner* (1982), with its constantly dark and rainy futuristic cityscapes.

The track was originally released on 1989's *Tarquin's Seaweed Farm* cassette and lent its title to a compilation of 'rare and early tracks' from the Porcupine Tree cassette days of 1989 to 1991, released in 1994 by Magic Gnome records. (See above).

Insignificance (1997)

Personnel:
Steven Wilson: all instruments and vocals
Release date: March 1997
Record label: Delerium
Current release: Currently unavailable, except as part of the thirteen-CD box set *The Delerium Years 1991-1997*.

This collection of Steven Wilson's demos for *Signify* (1996) was originally released only to subscribers to the band's Transmission information service in 1997. In 2003, it was released as the second disc of the remastered *Signify*. It includes a few formative versions of tracks that appeared on the final album and several tracks that didn't make the final cut.

'Wake As Gun I' (3:29)

A fragile, melancholy song featuring acoustic guitar, glowing synth lines, and what sounds like a hammered dulcimer (see entry on 'Lips of Ashes' from *In Absentia*). It appears to be about the search for significance in life, one of the main themes of *Signify*. Music is described as a force that liberates calm, just as the song itself does. The lyrics contain a clever conceit: that of a man waking up as a different entity in different scenarios: the most cynical of which is the one that gives the song its title: 'Man wakes up as a gun/And doesn't get the joke'; the protagonist fails to appreciate the irony of dedicating his life to violence. The opening guitar chords are also used in the song 'Jack the Sax' – from the 1997 No-Man album *Dry Cleaning Ray* – which had a completely different lyric, written and sung by Steven's No-Man partner, Tim Bowness.

'Hallogallo' (3.37)

A cover version of 'Hallogallo' by Neu!. For more detail, see the entry for the *Signify* title track.

'Smiling Not Smiling' (3:49)

One of several Porcupine Tree songs in which there is cognitive dissonance between the lyric's dystopian world-view, and the music's gentle qualities. It describes what could be an impending nuclear war: 'a ticking bomb of bone and thin air', with, at times, a folky quality sounding like Syd Barrett, and some nicely Floydian slide guitar.

'Wake As Gun II' (2:06)
Begins with a short reprise of part one (see above) before a brief free-form instrumental section.

'Neural Rust' (5:53)
This instrumental takes its name from the 'Every Home Is Wired' lyric line: 'Hit the solvent keypad/Start the neural rust.' Being a strong song, if it had been recorded by the whole band, it could've made it onto *Signify*. It begins with an excellent bass line, joined by lead guitar in unison, leading to a section of syncopated keyboards and then a breakdown: when a lovely, slightly discordant flute part appears, as the drums drop out. The inventive middle eight has a very satisfying chord sequence.

'Dark Origins' (6:54)
Another instrumental, but very different from the previous one. Unusually for a Porcupine Tree song, it remains on the same chord throughout, although an added bass line near the end creates a little variety. It's trance-like in its repeated musical mantra, with bluesy, spacey guitar riffs and a wordless female vocal.

'Sever Tomorrow' (6:04)
This is very similar to the final version (renamed 'Sever' on the studio album) and shows how fully developed many of Steven's demos were.

Metanoia (1998)
Personnel:
Steven Wilson: guitar and keyboards
Richard Barbieri: synthesisers
Colin Edwin: fretless bass
Chris Maitland: drums
Record label: Chromatic Records
Release date: December 1998
Current edition: part of the thirteen-CD box set *The Delerium Years 1991-1997*, and on streaming services

A collection of instrumental improvisations, recorded during the *Signify* sessions in 1995 and 1996, and originally released as a limited edition of 1,000 copies. The 2001 CD edition was limited to 5,000 copies, adding 'Insignificance' and 'Door to the River', originally included on 1997's *Insignificance*, but more logically belonging here. All songs were written and recorded by the full band. The CD booklet said, 'We made it up as we went along'. The album has a spacey, airy, sometimes psychedelic feel, with trance-like repetition and long-form improvisation. It's a good showcase for the band's many strengths: Steven Wilson's extended guitar soloing; Richard Barbieri's atmospheric and sometimes glittering keyboards; Chris Maitland's syncopated and fierce drumming, and Colin Edwin's funky fretless bass, which is an album highlight. Everything is beautifully recorded and mixed.

'Mesmer I' (8:33)
The German physician, Franz Mesmer, is most famous for mesmerism, which has become synonymous with hypnotism. This and the following two tracks are hypnotic – or mesmeric – in their repetition.

'Mesmer II' (6:05)
Notable for its opening Robert Fripp-style guitar, some languid drumming and Colin Edwin's excellent bass-playing.

'Mesmer III/Coma Divine' (13:18)
The third part has a spoken-word introduction, beginning with studio chat. This leads to the sound of browsing across radio stations, like the opening of Pink Floyd's 'Wish You Were Here'. Then there's a short section mixing radio chatter with orchestral music, not unlike part of 'Revolution 9': John Lennon's avant-garde sound collage on *The Beatles* (1968). The improvisation continues, notable for Chris Maitland's superb drumming.

'Door to the River' (4:08)
This relatively short track features echoey synths, heavy use of fretless bass harmonics, sporadic piano chords and distant, distorted guitars.

'Metanoia I/Intermediate Jesus' (14:14)
The title seems to relate to some of the main studio albums' religious themes: metanoia is a change in lifestyle following a spiritual conversion; 'Intermediate Jesus' is a *Signify* track featuring a passionate preacher. But it is in fact, an instrumental, which seems to have no thematic meaning. Like 'Coma Divine' (the name of a live album) and 'Insignificance' (the name of a compilation) (both from this album), this instrumental seems included to relate to other parts of the Porcupine Tree universe. The track, along with the next two, forms part of a continuous suite. It begins with a quiet storm of electronics, and like the next two tracks, is notable for a repeated bass riff.

'Insignificance' (4:56)
This section has the same feel as the suite's first part and builds to a climax with fiercely virtuosic drumming from Chris Maitland: featuring some pulsating double-kick pedal work towards the end.

'Metanoia II' (10:58)

Opening with even more stormy electronics, some lovely instrumental interplay around five minutes in is gradually swamped by Richard Barbieri's synth chords. The guitar lines become more fractured and the track speeds to a climax, gaining momentum before grinding to a halt as if the tape has suddenly been switched off.

'Milan' (2:27)

This spoken-word track consists of the band chatting about their choice of food at a restaurant in Milan. Voices of individual band members drift in and out of the mix in a free-form style, just as their instrumental voices do on the album's other tracks.

Voyage 34 (1992, 1993 and 2000)

Personnel:
Steven Wilson: programming, production and performance
Richard Barbieri: synthesizers on 'Phase IV'
Recorded at No Man's Land, June – July 1992; 'Phase IV' recorded in August 1993
Remix and additional production of 'Phase IV': Swordfish for Astralasia, August 1993
Release date: as a single ('Phase I' and 'Phase II'): November 1992; As an EP (Phase III and Phase IV): November 1993; as a compilation ('Phases I – IV') under the title *Voyage 34: The Complete Trip*: 2000
Chart placings: Did not chart
Running time: 'Phase I' (12:57), 'Phase II' (17:30), 'Phase III' (19:29), 'Phase IV' (19:47) (Timings vary in different versions)
Record label: Delerium
Current edition: Kscope

Porcupine Tree's second album, *Up the Downstair,* was originally to be a double album (like the debut, *On the Sunday of Life*), including this track. Steven said on the band's site that he couldn't 'remember the exact reason' why the album was trimmed down to one 48-minute disc without 'Voyage 34', but it might've been 'something to do with the fact that the double album had been so expensive to make and to get people to listen to'.

'Phase III' on *Voyage 34: Remixes (Phase III and IV)*, was remixed by Astralasia: described on their website as 'Early creators of original Euphoric Trance, Psychedelic Trance, Astral Dub, Trance, Experimantal (sic) Techno, Ambient Dance'. The mix is much more ambient and downtempo than the previous versions, leading the listener into a dreamlike state. The same can be said of 'Phase IV': remixed by Steven himself, with Richard Barbieri on keyboards.

The original single and the remixes were collected together in 2000 under the title *Voyage 34: The Complete Trip*.

The 'Voyage 34' story is based on a bad LSD trip. The spoken-word samples are taken from a documentary album called *LSD,* which was released on vinyl in America in 1966. The album describes itself, rather excitedly, as 'a documentary report on the current psychedelic drug controversy!' It promises to include 'actual recordings of people under the influence of psychedelic drugs'. But despite this somewhat voyeuristic approach, the recording features one of the most prominent medical experts on the dangers of psychedelic drugs: Dr Sidney Cohen. It was Cohen who, in the early 1960s, became concerned with the recreational use of LSD. He conducted experiments into the drug's safe use as a tool in a therapeutic setting under close medical supervision. He later grew concerned about the drug's dangers even when used in a medical context. It's *his* voice we hear describing the effect of the bad trip on 'Brian', whose progress is followed over a twelve-hour period in the documentary: 'This young man never had a bummer in some 33 LSD trips. Every one of them was a delight, everything under control. He needed only to snap his fingers and down he came, anytime. But on voyage 34, he finally met himself coming down an up-staircase, and the encounter was crushing.'

It was Richard Allen – Delerium Records owner and later Porcupine Tree manager – who gave Steven Wilson a copy of the LP, suggesting it could provide musical inspiration. Steven told Stephen Humphries in the notes for the box set *Porcupine Tree: The Delerium Years 1991-1997* that, although the LP is presented as a documentary, 'It is clearly staged. It was basically propaganda that was created to dissuade kids from taking LSD. Although the whole thing is presented as real, it does smack of being scripted. I think that's part of the appeal of it. There's something very kitschy about that. It was crying out to be set to music.'

Whatever the nature of the documentary itself, Steven was right about the album narration's dramatic effect. Even this early in his songwriting career, he could see the narrative structure that the 34th trip description would provide, and he imaginatively stripped out the recorded excerpts of Brian's incoherent trip babblings, leaving only some of his maniacal laughter. The music, therefore, replaces Brian's speech, leaving only the slightly sinister commentary describing Brian's bad trip: a narrative drive matched by Steven's propulsive electronic techno laced with lysergic guitars.

Richard Allen designed the single cover, which is closely based on the sleeve of another 1960s record: *L.S.D.* by Dr. Timothy Leary Ph.D. Leary famously used the phrase 'Turn on, tune in, drop out' in 1967 at a gathering of 30,000 hippies. Years later, in his autobiography (*Flashbacks, A Personal and Cultural History of an Era*), he said 'turn on' meant 'activate your neural and genetic equipment'; 'tune in' meant 'interact harmoniously with the world around you'; and 'drop out' meant 'self-reliance, a discovery of one's singularity, a commitment to mobility, choice, and change'. He denied that he'd meant 'Get stoned and abandon all constructive activity', but thousands in America and elsewhere embraced that message. Allen took the day-glo, swirling optical illusion in red and yellow from Leary's album cover, instead using green and blue on the 'Voyage 34' cover. Later versions made the drug reference more explicit, with three tablets floating against a blue background.

The back cover of the *L.S.D.* album, poses a series of questions, such as, 'How should psychedelic drugs be used?', and 'Is LSD habit-forming?'. Richard Allen wittily replaced these questions on the single's back cover with 'How should Porcupine Tree be used' and 'Is Porcupine Tree habit forming'. (Many fans would answer 'yes' to the latter). A sticker on the single cover, read 'A post-rave space wave to the Darkside of the Moon. After listening to this recording, your friends won't know you anymore. You're on Voyage 34 now – Hallelujah!'

The sticker also read, 'Warning – Over 30 minutes long'. It remains one of the longest singles ever released, beaten only by The Orb's 1992 single, 'Blue Room', which at 39:57, is just below the maximum limit of 40 minutes that qualifies music for single length. On the Porcupine Tree site, Steven admitted his musical debt to The Orb: 'This was the era of ambient music, and The Orb were the name to drop. I liked what they were doing but wanted to try and fuse it with the guitar on a very long piece.'

The guitar part owes an obvious debt to Pink Floyd: in particular, 'Another Brick in the Wall, Part I' ('Daddy's flown across the ocean...') from *The Wall* (1979). But Steven said the real influence was Ash Ra Tempel's 1975 ambient album, *Inventions for Electric Guitar*, performed by guitarist and composer Manuel Göttsching, a major figure in the German kosmische musik movement. Having said that, Steven did tell Stephen Humphries that he used a 'David Gilmour-like guitar pattern' as the track's anchor.

'Voyage 34' was an experiment in genre, as Steven told Tushar Menon in the June 2012 edition of *Rolling Stone India*: 'Back in the early '90s, there was an explosion in ambient music: a fusion of electronic music and techno music with the philosophy of people like Brian Eno and Tangerine Dream. I thought there was an interesting opportunity to do something that would bring progressive rock and psychedelia into that mixture.'

The track contains an ambient sample from the Van Der Graaf Generator epic, 'A Plague of Lighthouse Keepers' (from *Pawn Hearts*, 1971). The sample comes from the song's second section, 'Pictures/Lighthouse': written by saxophonist/flautist David Jackson and organist Hugh Banton. Appropriately enough, that piece includes the line, 'I'm so far out I'm too far in': suggesting paradoxically that the protagonist is meeting himself coming back, just like Brian on his 34th voyage.

'Voyage 34' also samples the opening of 'As the Bell Rings the Maypole Spins', from the 1990 *Aion* album by Australian art rock duo, Dead Can Dance. Lisa Gerrard sings the words (in a made-up language) 'Ka uni tramaya', to medieval-sounding music. (Steven also references that band – along with Felt and This Mortal Coil – on his *Hand. Cannot. Erase.* track, 'Perfect Life' (2015).

'Voyage 34' became, in Steven's words. 'a big indie cult hit, and really put Porcupine Tree on the map'. It reached number 18 in the *NME* (*New Musical Express*) indie chart and took on a life of its own when played in nightclubs.

Richard Allen told Stephen Humphries that he met a girl at London's Marquee club, who was amazed how accurately the track recreated the experience of an LSD trip. He didn't have the heart to tell her that Steven 'hadn't touched anything stronger than a glass of wine'.

The song was the first that Porcupine Tree ever played live: in December 1993, at their first gig. Decades later – in December 2020 – Steven posted a YouTube video of the song, in a version lasting only about six minutes, saying that, 'This session version is much abbreviated, but look out for a more extended updating of Brian's 34th LSD trip, on my tour next year'.

Recordings (2001)

Personnel:
Steven Wilson: vocals, guitars, pianos, samples, hammered dulcimer, Mellotron
Richard Barbieri: keyboards and analogue synthesizers
Chris Maitland: drums
Colin Edwin: bass and double bass
Strings: East of England Orchestra conducted by Nicholas Kok
Theo Travis: saxophone, flute
Release date: May 2001
Record label: Kscope
Current edition: Transmission re-release, bandcamp.com and streaming

Recordings was originally compiled in 2000 to help finance a tour and is made up of songs from the *Stupid Dream/Lightbulb Sun* era. The first two tracks were previously unreleased, and the rest mostly appeared as CD single B-sides. The original release was limited to 20,000. Some songs didn't qualify for original albums because they didn't really fit: not due to lack of quality. According to the band's website, 'The band and many fans consider it to be every bit as strong as (*Stupid Dream* and *Lightbulb Sun)'*.

'Buying New Soul' (Richard Barbieri, Colin Edwin, Chris Maitland, Steven Wilson) (10:24)
This track was recorded in writing sessions at Foel Studios, Wales, in March 2000, just after *Lightbulb Sun* was completed. It's a gorgeous, poignant song with a haunting chorus that could've easily earned a place on one of the main studio albums. It follows the Stupid Dream theme: the difficulty of balancing artistic integrity and commercial success. A highly personal song, it reflects Steven's continuing fight against the music industry – 'I still rage and wage my little war' – but it ends with the depressing concept of selling out, of buying a 'new soul at the start of every year'. The circling synthesizer motif that opens and closes the song perfectly matches the melancholy lyric and jazz-like upright bass. There is one moment of rage, but the feeling is generally one of resignation. For listeners familiar with only the band's main albums, 'Buying New Soul' is an undiscovered gem.

'Access Denied' (3:35)

A previously unreleased demo from the *Lightbulb Sun* sessions. Except for Steven, the band didn't like it but relented this time. Steven plays hammered dulcimer on this track and 'In Formaldehyde'.

A strange song that breaks the spell of the previous track somewhat, it begins with a 1960s pastiche feel, similar to 'Piano Lesson' from *Stupid Dream*. It's not clear what it's about, although it does contain the excellent, deeply ironic lines: 'Don't want to smother you/Just want you to be the mother of my children.'

'Cure for Optimism' (6:11)

This track from the 'Shesmovedon' CD single (2000), is a Steven Wilson solo performance at his home studio. It's another song where the meaning is just out of reach, but the track is still very evocative, with ghostly echoed piano motifs and subtle acoustic guitars. Mental health appears to be a theme here. The reference to a 'serpent on a mobile phone' could suggest a record company executive. Another hidden gem.

'Untitled' (Richard Barbieri, Colin Edwin, Chris Maitland, Steven Wilson) (8:53)

From the 'Shesmovedon' CD single; a live band improvisation recorded at Foel studios. It begins with gentle bowed double-bass notes – like the start of 'Buying New Soul' – which morph into plucked notes. The track demonstrates the band's ability to improvise expressive soundscapes rather than exhibit virtuosity, as they often do on instrumentals elsewhere.

'Disappear' (3:37)

From the 'Four Chords That Made a Million' CD single (2000); recorded during the *Lightbulb Sun* sessions. Another meditation on the theme of fame, with the plaintive lyric, 'I've got a voice inside me saying give it up ... You'll be famous, I'll disappear': much more subtle than the single's title track.

'Ambulance Chasing' (Richard Barbieri, Colin Edwin, Chris Maitland, Steven Wilson) (6:32)

Another instrumental, which appeared on the 'Piano Lessons' CD single (1999); recorded during the *Stupid Dream* sessions. It begins with thunderous drums, sounding like those in King Crimson's 'B'Boom' from *Thrak* (1995) or *The Flowers of Romance* (1981) by Public Image Ltd. A deliberately off-key keyboard motif, gives the feel of horror film music before the track switches to a mellifluous chord sequence. Eventually, the sound fractures before a powerful drum break introduces an extended guitar solo. It's a very satisfying track, in some ways better than 'Piano Lessons', though perhaps less immediate.

'In Formaldehyde' (5:19)

From the 'Four Chords That Made a Million' CD single (2000); recorded during the *Lightbulb Sun* sessions. This is another track that could fall into the 'divorce songs' category: a major theme of *Lightbulb Sun*. As so often happens in Porcupine Tree songs, Steven creates beauty out of melancholy and bitterness. The relationship's inequality is encapsulated in the split's material outcome: 'I get a plastic vase/And you get to keep the car.'

'Oceans Have No Memory' (3:06)

Steven's demo version appeared as the B-side of the 'Piano Lessons' 7" single (1999). But this is a new full-band version: a contemplative instrumental, reminiscent of Fleetwood Mac's 'Albatross' (1968).

Stars Die: The Delerium Years 1991-1997 (2002)

Personnel: See chapters on albums listed below for details
Release date: March 2002
Label: Kscope
Current edition: bandcamp.com and streaming

This compilation includes tracks from the Delerium albums: *On the Sunday of Life* ('Radioactive Toy', 'Nine Cats', 'And the Swallows Dance Above The Sun', 'Nostalgia Factory'); *Voyage 34* ('Phase One'); *Up the Downstair* ('Synesthesia', 'Up the Downstair', 'Fadeaway'); *Staircase Infinities* ('Rainy Taxi'); *The Sky Moves Sideways* ('Stars Die' (US version), 'Phase One'); *Signify* ('Waiting', 'Every Home Is Wired', 'Sever', 'Dark Matter'). Additional tracks are listed below, and quotes from Steven and the band are taken from the sleeve notes. This album is highly recommended as an introduction to early Porcupine Tree.

'Phantoms' (Alan Duffy, Steven Wilson) (3:17)

An out-take from *Up the Downstair*. Steven said he left it off that album because he was uncomfortable with his voice sounding 'very exposed' but later changed his mind. He also said the song was written in a Syd Barrett way, with 'lots of sections joined together in a very singer-songwritery manner'. The vocal stands up well; the words, confessional: 'And I'm sorry I treat you this way'. Perhaps what Steven had identified was the slight unease between Alan Duffy's mildly psychedelic lyrics and Steven's own emotionally raw performance: a problem he was able to avoid later by writing all his own lyrics.

'Men of Wood' (Alan Duffy, Steven Wilson) (3:35)

Previously unreleased. Steven said he found it difficult to find a home for this track. It was considered for two albums and as a single but didn't quite fit the band's changing style: 'It was almost a throwback to (the band's) psychedelic pop, and that just wasn't quite right – it was a context thing.'

The theme is the vacuity of modern society: sharing a sentiment with T. S. Eliot's poem, 'The Hollow Men'. The song begins with a dirty sounding guitar, then heads for a memorable chorus with a nicely psychedelic key-change, giving it a rather wistful feel.

'The Sound of No-One Listening' (8:13)

This instrumental track was cut from *Signify* because 'the band considered it to be closer to the ethos of *The Sky Move Sideways*', despite its 'driving power'. It appeared as the B-side of the 'Waiting' CD single (1996).

The track starts with ominous soundscaping and sound effects, including the sound of an ice cream van: which has become a common horror film trope, though it may have a sense of nostalgia for some listeners. Although the band may have changed style by the time it was recorded, it's an excellent track that stands up very well in retrospect, with a simple compelling bass riff and the same lovely flute motif used in 'Neural Rust'. Synth arpeggios provide a glittering, hopeful backdrop, as the song reaches a climax with very energetic drumming before falling back into a darkly disturbing noise-scape again.

'Colourflow in Mind' (3:49)

Appeared on the B-side of the 'Waiting' 7" single. Steven said, 'None of the band liked it! I thought it was a great track.' When he played them the demo, they were all bored by it, but they relented sufficiently to allow it onto this compilation.

The song appears to be about taking drugs: particularly as it references Dr. Timothy Leary's famous phrase, 'Turn on, tune in, drop out', with the line 'Turn on, tune in, shut down'. (For a discussion of Timothy Leary and LSD, see the section on *Voyage 34*).

'Fuse the Sky' (4:33)

This track is also from the 'Waiting' 7" single. It began life as a remix of 'The Colour of Air': the opening section of 'The Sky Moves Sideways'. *Volume* magazine had asked for something 'ambient and trancey' for a cover CD, but they turned it down.

'Signify II' (6:04)

This instrumental was left off *Signify* to ensure a 'more ear-friendly running time'. There was also concern that it harked back to the prog styles of *The Sky Moves Sideways* with its 'progressive rock time-signature tricks'. (For further discussion, see the reference to 'Signify' in the *Signify* chapter).

Deadwing (Bonus tracks) (2005)

Personnel: See *Deadwing*
Release date: May 2005
Current edition: unavailable

The tracks below were issued as bonus tracks with the DVD-Audio version of *Deadwing*. Live versions can be found on the *Arriving Somewhere...* CD/ DVD ('Revenant', 'Mother And Child Divided', 'So Called Friend') and the *Anesthetize* CD/DVD ('Half-Light').

'Revenant' (Barbieri) 3:04

A Richard Barbieri instrumental, using the same electric piano sound as 'My Ashes' from *Fear of a Blank Planet*. It's a thoughtful, subtle track, highlighting Barbieri's rich keyboard textures. Gentle guitar and tasteful percussion complete the picture, creating a lovely miniature.

'Mother and Child Divided' (Gavin Harrison, Steven Wilson) (5:03)

Mother and Child Divided is the name of a sculpture by English artist Damien Hirst. It consists of four tanks containing a cow and a calf, each cut in half. This instrumental track features co-writer Gavin Harrison's superb drumming and a rising, chromatic guitar melody. The guitar riff at around 2:30 is also used on 'Halo' from the main *Deadwing* album, albeit in a different key.

'Half-Light' (6:20)

This feels like a companion track to 'Lazarus' from the main album: the link strengthened by the whispered name 'David' at around twenty seconds in. David is the *Deadwing* film script's central character (see the *Deadwing* chapter for details). Like 'Lazarus', it has a wistful lyricism, perfectly expressed through Steven's soulful vocal. It seems to share the 'Lazarus' theme, both in the moonlit (or half-lit) setting, and the idea of leaving: 'Come to us, Lazarus/ It's time for you to go' ... 'I will go now/But I will be with you.'

'So Called Friend' (Richard Barbieri, Colin Edwin, Gavin Harrison, Steven Wilson) (4:49)

This has a funky swagger about it, with a touch of heavy metal drive, similar in feel to 'Nil Recurring' (See below). The vitriolic chorus sums up the song's bitterness: 'Sleep well my so-called friend, a virus in your heart/She bends, my so-called friend and rips my life apart.'

Nil Recurring (2007)

Personnel:
Steven Wilson: vocals, guitars, keyboards
Richard Barbieri: keyboards and synthesizers
Colin Edwin: bass
Gavin Harrison: drums, percussion, tapped guitar on 'Nil Recurring'
Robert Fripp: lead guitar on 'Nil Recurring'
Ben Coleman: electric violin on 'What Happens Now?'

Recorded at No Man's Land, Bourne Place, New Rising, The Artillery, Nightspace, Red Room Recorders, DGM – October-December 2006 and July 2007
Produced and arranged by: Porcupine Tree
Release date: UK: September 2007, USA: February 2008
Chart placings: UK Indie: 8, USA: Did not chart
Running time: 28:44
Record label: Transmission (UK) Peaceville (USA)

Nil Recurring is a collection of tracks left off *Fear of a Blank Planet*. This doesn't necessarily mean they are inferior to the songs on that album; the material here is very strong, and Steven decided that it deserved to be released in the form of a separate EP, rather than as bonus tracks.

'Nil Recurring' (Richard Barbieri, Colin Edwin, Gavin Harrison, Steven Wilson) (6:08)

This instrumental features King Crimson's Robert Fripp on lead guitar (see the notes on 'Way Out of Here' from *Fear of a Blank Planet* for more detail). In 2010, Steven told Anil Prasad of *Innerviews.org* that Fripp was a huge influence on his guitar-soloing philosophy: 'It's based on the Robert Fripp approach: play the notes with conviction but don't think too hard about what you're playing. Also, play as few notes as possible with as much emotion as possible.'

After two minutes of guitar tapping (played by drummer Gavin Harrison) and heavy riffing, a lovely, spacious breakdown highlights Colin Edwin's bass and Richard Barbieri's keyboards. Then, at around 3:20, the track gathers momentum, and a lovely riff cuts across a punchy one-note bass section. At around five minutes in, the opening echoed tapped-guitar theme, returns, with a manic guitar solo and further heavy riffing, until the track suddenly dissolves.

'Normal' (Steven Wilson) (7:08)

This track shares the line, 'I do a good impression of myself', with 'Anesthetize', and it shares the chorus of 'Sentimental' (Both from *Fear of a Blank Planet*).

The protagonist is not the teenage boy character from *Fear of a Blank Planet*; he is an adult who owns a car, a phone and a TV; but like the protagonist in 'What Happens Now' (see below), these possessions mean little to him, and he's in a state of existential crisis: '... am I here? It's kind of hard to tell'. He also seems to have a great deal in common with the adult narrator of *Lunar Park,* the Bret Easton Ellis novel that inspired the main album; he struggles to 'get through the day' without drugs. If that seems like unusual behaviour, the response is 'What's normal now, anyway?'.

'Cheating the Polygraph' (Gavin Harrison, Steven Wilson) (7:06)

Gavin Harrison performed a completely different big-band version of this on his 2015 solo album of the same name.

The song's sentiment is very simple: the protagonist has learned to lie so well that he can cheat a lie detector. He tells lies to his partner – not the small white lies that help to keep a relationship on track; these lies are 'black'. His lies are so bad that he is 'blackening my soul'. At the end, he shows a degree of remorse for once: 'God, I'm so ashamed, this time.' But we probably no longer believe him as he is evidently such an accomplished liar.

The verses – sung in a relaxed, almost disingenuous style – suggest the protagonist has accepted the need to lie and is fairly relaxed about it. But the chorus shows the true extent of his anguish: sounding distorted and strained as he feels his soul going colder.

At around four minutes in, a guitar wails above a simple repetitive bass line. Soon comes a moment of respite, where the drums drop out and the gentle synth textures suggest sympathy for the protagonist, and that perhaps he does have a soul after all: just as in *Fear of a Blank Planet*. That album's echoes are confirmed through the 'Anesthetize' instrumental quotes.

This is a mini-epic, expressing several emotions in a fairly short space of time.

'What Happens Now?' (Richard Barbieri, Colin Edwin, Gavin Harrison, Steven Wilson) (8:24)

This song's protagonist seems to be suffering an existential crisis, rather like the main character in *Fear of a Blank Planet*. Material possessions mean nothing to him and they bore him: 'So I got all these things, but so what?' As he says, 'You can't take them with you', and instead, he seeks meaning through religion, asking the song's mystery addressee: 'You think you can save my soul?' The answer – given in verse 2 – seems to be that he could die as a result of a suicide bombing, although the link between verses one and two is oblique. He boards a plane, in which somebody has concealed a bomb in a briefcase: as a result of which, 'My body will spread through the heavens, across the sky/And my ashes will fall through the cloudburst.' It's a surprising and poetic image, despite its bleak suggestion that the answer is oblivion. The words 'my ashes', recall the song of that name from *Fear of a Blank Planet*.

Instrumentally, the track is again very strong. Of particular note, is the rhythmic illusion: beginning at about five minutes in, becoming much clearer at around 6:00, when the drums appear to move at half the speed of the other instruments, before the whole track slows down to an epic feeling of finality.

In Absentia (Deluxe Edition) (2020)

Personnel: See *In Absentia*
Release Date: 28 February 2020
Record Label: Kscope (Box set) and streaming services

This version of *In Absentia* is available as a three-CD/one-DVD box set, and on streaming services. It contains a remastered version, demos of several tracks, and the following additional recordings.

'Collapse Intro' (01:45)

The intro to the main album's final track includes additional lyrics, making it an even more bitter break-up song: 'I won't bleed when you bite/But I'll still crawl back to you/Through the hate and the spite.'

'Drown With Me' (05:21)

In the interview filmed for the *In Absentia* Deluxe Edition of 2020, Steven Wilson told Lasse Hoile that he thought this song was going to be 'one of the highlights' of the album. He replaced it with 'Prodigal', 'which I think is one of the weaker songs', although he stressed this was a very personal opinion that others might disagree with. The reason for the substitution was that he felt 'Prodigal' was a better recording, although he regretted the decision later.

'Drown With Me' is a gorgeous, upbeat song in which the music contrasts sharply with the lyrics. We're back in the main album's world of serial killers: referring to the protagonist's plan to drown the song's addressee and her family. As in 'Blackest Eyes', the victim is enticed into the killer's violent world. Compare 'Swim with me into your blackest eyes' with 'You should drown with me'.

'Orchidia' (03:27)

This and the next two tracks were released on the 2003 *Futile* promo EP. 'Orchidia' is a lively, tuneful instrumental with some unexpected key changes. It could've easily made it onto the main album with some polishing and additional soundscaping.

'Chloroform' (Chris Maitland, Steven Wilson) (7:14)

This song's co-writer – drummer Chris Maitland – left the band just before *In Absentia* was recorded, so it was perhaps politically expedient to leave it off the album. To be fair, the drum rhythm is excellent and is well-matched with Colin Edwin's upright electric bass. The track also features an uplifting guitar solo, and a subtly atmospheric final keyboard section, in a minor key. Lyrically, it's rather surreal, perhaps because we may be experiencing things from the drowsy, confused state of someone who's inhaled chloroform: 'Speak clearer, can't hear you, I'm going under.' Whether the album's serial killer administered the chloroform is left to our imagination.

'Futile' (Gavin Harrison, Steven Wilson) (6:06)

This is the strongest example of the band's interest in the music of Swedish heavy metal band, Meshuggah. Gavin Harrison told Lasse Hoile that he wanted to write a Meshuggah-inspired track, that he could use as a challenge in at his drum clinics, as he was finding it hard to play heavy metal. He invited Steven to add guitar parts to the demo, resulting in 'one of the heaviest pieces we ever recorded'.

Lyrically, we may be back in the world of the serial killer: 'You were the one that made her cry ... the world went black ... lost my head.' The chorus is fiercely dark: the metallic guitars almost burying the vocals. What makes the song remarkable is the contrast of the main guitar riff's ferocity with the yearning delicacy of the backing vocals.

'Meantime' (3:17)

A simple, folky song with rich harmonies. Although Steven's voice sounds a little tired at times, it does provide emotional rawness and honesty. The track fits with the wider *In Absentia* theme: an absence; a failure to connect emotionally with the outside world, which the protagonist views as if on a 3D TV screen: 'Maybe it's just living gets me down/Three dimensions, realistic sound.'

'Imogen Slaughter' (Demo) (2:38)

Steven Wilson described 'Imogen Slaughter' as a song that he loved, but one that would not have been right for *In Absentia*. He told Lasse Hoile it has a 'garage, trashy feel', a bit like Sonic Youth, with Richard Barbieri doing 'crazy electronic stuff'. Steven also thought the fans would've hated it, although he said that in itself, it would not have prevented him from putting it on the album.

'Watching You Sleep' (Demo) (3:44)

Steven called this a 'really pretty song' but said he was so unsure about it, he probably didn't even play it to the rest of the band. Later, he changed his mind: 'It's a good song ... people should hear it.' Perhaps his instinct was right. It is a good song, about childhood nostalgia, with images of endless summers and 'your weightless smile', but 'Trains' from the main album covers the topic more effectively.

'Enough' (Demo) (3:45)

This is a fascinating early version of what became a very different song. It's an almost visceral shock for the listener familiar with *In Absentia* to hear the opening words 'A mother sings a lullaby to a child' in the context of 'Enough': a well-crafted indie rock song. The song became 'Blackest Eyes'. 'Enough' also features the words, 'It's so erotic when your make-up fails'; on 'Blackest Eyes' the final word is 'runs' rather than 'fails': a much more potent image – the make-up 'runs' due to tears of pain or horror. An excellent example of how a good song turned into a great one.

Porcupine Tree: The Delerium Years 1991-1997 (2020)

A deluxe limited edition thirteen-CD box set compiling all the band's recordings issued by the Delerium label between 1992 and 1997. It consists of the studio albums – *On the Sunday of Life, Up the Downstair, The Sky Moves Sideways, Signify* – and the live album, *Coma Divine*. It also includes *Voyage 34: The Complete Trip* (with the original full-length version of Phase IV) and remastered versions of *Staircase Infinities* and *Metanoia*. There's an unedited version of the 'Moonloop' improvisation from *The Sky Moves Sideways*, under the name *Transmission IV*.

Finally, there are two compilations: *Insignificance* (see above) and a new compilation – *The Sound of No One Listening* – which rounds up stray single and compilation tracks which had appeared elsewhere, and includes two demo versions of 'Disappear' (a shorter version of the track can be found on *Recordings*). *The Sound of No One Listening* is now available on streaming services.

EPs
Moonloop (1994) – See chapter on *The Sky Moves Sideways*
Coma Divine II (1999) – Released as a promo CD for the live *Coma Divine* album. The tracks were incorporated into later versions of the main album.
Transmission IV (2001) – See above; now available on streaming services
Futile (2003) – a promo CD for *In Absentia*. The tracks were released as part of that album's deluxe edition in 2020.
Pure Narcotic (2020) – An acoustic set recorded in the studio after experiencing technical problems recording at the Royal Albert Hall, London, in October 2010. The 2020 vinyl edition sold out, but the EP is available on bandcamp.com.

Singles
Voyage 34 (1992) – See above
Stars Die (1995) – See *The Sky Moves Sideways*
Waiting (1996) – See *Signify*
Piano Lessons, Stranger by the Minute, Pure Narcotic (1999) – See *Stupid Dream*
Four Chords That Made a Million, Shesmovedon (2000) – See *Lightbulb Sun*
Lazarus, Shallow (2005) – See *Deadwing*

Live Albums

Coma Divine (CD) (1997)

Recorded over the three nights of 25-27 March 1997, at Frontiera in Rome, before a capacity crowd. This marked the end of the era when the band was still largely a vehicle for Steven Wilson's solo – and often largely instrumental – songs. It was also the last album recorded before the band parted with Delerium Records. According to the band's website: 'The only overdubs on the album were the vocals, which for technical and performance reasons, had to be done again.'

The material is drawn from the band's first four albums: *On the Sunday of Life*, *Up the Downstair*, *The Sky Moves Sideways* and *Signify*. The original single CD release contained ten tracks, and the 2003 remaster was a double CD with four additional tracks. Intriguingly, a full-length version of 'Voyage 34' was recorded but not released, as was a new track 'Cryogenics' (written especially for the album) which Steven regarded as 'frankly, poor'. This is the only main live album to feature Chris Maitland on drums.

Arriving Somewhere... (CD/DVD) (2006)

In August 2006, the band's website excitedly announced: 'Finally a live performance DVD by Porcupine Tree!'. It was filmed on the *Deadwing* tour at Park West, Chicago, in October 2005, edited by Lasse Hoile, and mixed in stereo and 5.1 surround sound by Steven Wilson. The original two-disc release came with a bonus disc that included 'Futile' and 'Radioactive Toy', recorded on the German TV show *Rockpalast*. The album consists of several tracks from *Deadwing*, four from *In Absentia*, and a couple each from *Lightbulb Sun* and *Stupid Dream*. It's the first of the main live albums to feature Gavin Harrison on drums and John Wesley on guitar and backing vocals: as all the subsequent ones did.

Anesthetize (CD/DVD) (2010)

Filmed over two nights in Tilburg, Netherlands, in October 2008, at the end of the *Fear of a Blank Planet* tour. It features a complete performance of that album. There are also tracks from *Signify*, *In Absentia*, *Nil Recurring*, and *Deadwing*. The DVD was filmed in HD, directed and edited by Lasse Hoile. Many of the shots are filmed from behind Gavin Harrison's drum kit, giving a real insight into his skill and virtuosity. Quoted on the band's website, Jerry Ewing from *Prog* magazine praised 'the sumptuous sound and spot-on performance'.

Atlanta (Download) (2010)

Another (audio only) recording from the *Fear of a Blank Planet* tour. It was recorded in October 2007 at the Roxy Theatre, Atlanta, and mixed for CD release; but remained in the vault when the decision was made to record and film other dates from the tour (see above). The recording was eventually released as a download only to raise funds for Mick Karn's cancer treatment (Karn was the bassist for Japan, for whom Richard Barbieri played keyboards). His appeal for financial help allowed him to return to London for treatment. Sadly, he died shortly after, in January 2011, aged 52. Proceeds from the album downloads now go to the Teenage Cancer Trust. The album is also available to stream. The tracklist is fairly similar to that of *Anesthetize*; with the addition of 'Open Car' (*Deadwing*), 'Blackest Eyes' (*In Absentia*), and the first official live recording of 'A Smart Kid' (*Stupid Dream*).

Octane Twisted (CD/DVD) (2012)

The last live recording by Porcupine Tree, this includes a complete performance of the song-cycle *The Incident*, recorded at The Riviera, Chicago, in April 2010. Also included, are 'Hatesong' and 'Russia on Ice' (*Lightbulb Sun*) (the latter combined with 'The Pills I'm Taking' (Part of 'Anesthetize' from *Fear of a Blank Planet*), 'Stars Die', and 'Bonnie the Cat' (*The Incident*). Three tracks were taken from the band's last ever live performance, at London's Royal Albert Hall on 14 October 2010: 'Even Less' (the extended version from *Recordings*), 'Dislocated Day' (*The Sky Moves Sideways*) and 'Arriving Somewhere but Not Here' (*Deadwing*).

Other Live Albums
Spiral Circus (1994)

Recorded at BBC studios, The Borderline in London, and The Nag's Head, High Wycombe, England. Limited release on cassette (1994) and vinyl (1997), now deleted.

Rockpalast (2006)

Audio from TV show at Live Music Hall in Cologne, Germany, 19 November 2005 – only available as a download.

Los Angeles House of Blues (2021)

A recording of the set played at the House of Blues, Los Angeles, on 30 July 2003, released as a limited edition in July 2021 on blue vinyl. The tour was shared with Opeth, who were joint headliners, and the album features the whole of Porcupine Tree's set except for 'Trains' in which a string broke. Tracks are taken from *In Absentia*, *Lightbulb Sun*, *Stupid Dream*, and *The Sky Moved Sideways*. In addition the band played 'Futile' the studio version of which featured in the Deluxe Edition of *In Absentia* (see above).

Bandcamp Downloads

In the spring of 2020, several of Porcupine's Tree live recordings were released on bandcamp.com as downloads, either individually or as a discounted set.

They are listed below in date order:

Nags Head, High Wycombe, England, 4 December 1993 – The band's first-ever live gig

Salford Chapman Theatre, Salford University, England, 2 November 1994

Coma: Code, Frontiera, Rome, Italy, 26th March 1997 – *Coma Divine* was recorded at the same time

Warszawa Polish Radio Program III, broadcast 6 April 2001; released on CD in 2004

XM, XM Satellite Radio Performance Studio One, Washington DC, USA, 12 November 2002

XMII, XM Satellite Radio Performance Studio One, Washington DC, USA, 21 July 2003

Los Angeles House of Blues, 30 July 2003; limited edition release on vinyl in July 2021 - see above

BBC Radio Session, Maida Vale Studios, London, England, 13 April 2007

Ilosaarirock, Ilosaarirock festival, Finland, 14 June 2007

We Lost The Skyline, In-store performance, Park Avenue, Orlando, Florida, 4 October 2007

Köln Palladium, Köln, Germany; Audio from show filmed by a local TV station, 4 December 2007

IndigO2, London, England, 19th Oct 2008

Acoustic Radio Session, Steven Wilson and John Wesley; Broadcast details lost/unknown, December 2009

Coda

Porcupine Tree began in 1987 as a bit of fun: a Steven Wilson solo project consisting of recordings made in his bedroom. It was meant to be a one-off, and he never had any real intention of seeking a record deal; even less of playing live. But nearly 25 years later, Porcupine Tree had become a successful band, able to fill London's Royal Albert Hall. Their albums had been nominated for Grammy awards, and the band were achieving chart success on both sides of the Atlantic.

More significant is the artistic journey the band took. Beginning with amusing psychedelic pastiches – like 'Linton Samuel Dawson' from the first album *On the Sunday of Life* – they ended up with the prog rock masterpiece, 'Anesthetize', from *Fear of a Blank Planet,* and a complete 55-minute song suite on the final album *The Incident*. Along the way were fascinating diversions, such as the fusion of prog rock and dance music: the epic single, 'Voyage 34'. There was also the sophisticated art rock and pop of albums like *Stupid Dream*.

The band's most important legacy is the creation of a new genre: a progressive rock and heavy metal hybrid, with ambient textures and strong melodies. This began with *In Absentia*, and continued with three more albums until the end of the band's career. Each of these albums – and some earlier ones too – could be regarded as *concept* albums, but if that conjures up images of the worst prog rock excesses, that would give the wrong impression. The concepts engage urgently and in a profound way, with some of the deepest issues of modern life: such as the effect of technology and prescription drugs on teenagers; the crucial 'incidents' that shape a life; and absence in the soul, experienced by the lonely, misfits, and those so alienated from society, that they become killers. These albums include short stories or vignettes contained in songs such as 'Heartattack in a Layby', and beautiful ballads such as 'Trains' and 'Lazarus'.

Although Steven Wilson wrote most of the music – and all of the lyrics after the early albums – the other musician's roles should not be underestimated. Excellent recording and production enhance the package, particularly on the later albums when the band were using major studios. But even in the early days, Steven achieved remarkable results in his home studio, No Man's Land, which he continued to use throughout the band's career. The final piece in the jigsaw was the photography of Lasse Hoile, who created the memorable, often disturbing images that translated Steven's thoughts into album and video visuals.

Finally, whether or not the label 'prog rock' is always appropriate for Porcupine Tree, the band played a major role in revitalising a genre that, to some, appeared to have become a relic of the past – a home for nostalgia, rather than the living art form it continues to be today.

Nick Holmes, Heaton Chapel, England 30 March 2021

Bibliography and References

General
porcupinetree.com (archived); relaunched and updated May 2021
stevenwilsonhq.com
SongMeanings.com
Tim Burgess' Twitter Listening Party @LISTENING_PARTY July 2020
Instagram @stevenwilsonhq
Notes by Stephen Humphries in the thirteen-CD box set *Porcupine Tree: The Delerium Years 1991-1997* (Transmission Recordings, 2020)
Notes in the two-CD compilation *Stars Die: The Delerium Years 1991–1997* (Kscope 2002)
Hoile, L., *Muzak: The Visual Art of Porcupine Tree* (Flood Gallery Publishing 2019)
Hoile, L., *The Making of In Absentia* (Documentary film from *In Absentia* deluxe edition 2020)

On the Sunday of Life
Allen, R., McMullen, P., *Porcupine Tree – Strange but True* (Terrascope.Com, 1996)
Clemons, P., *A chat with Steven Wilson late 1994* (Coventry Music Articles blogspot – republished 2017)
Crohinga Well Magazine #2, *Grantchester Meadows Revisited* (1992)
Thompson, J. , *Selection Section: 9 Key Records From Steven Wilson's Collection* (Discogs, 2017)
Keller, P., *Don't Hate Me: A Floyd Fan's Introduction to Porcupine Tree* (Spare Bricks/ Ministry of Information, undated)
Ling, D., *Steven Wilson and Richard Barbieri on the magic of Porcupine Tree* (Prog magazine, November 2016)
Rosen, S., *Steven Wilson: Porcupine Tree Was Gonna Be a One-Off Thing* (Ulimate-Guitar.com 2011)

Up the Downstair/Voyage 34/Staircase Infinities
Astralasia website – www.astralasia.co.uk
Dolan, E.W., *LSD alters the neural response to music in a number of brain regions, study finds* (PsyPost February 2020)
Laurence, A., *Porcupine Tree interview* (freewilliamsburg.com September 2002)
Leary, T., *Flashbacks: A Personal and Cultural History of an Era* (Jeremy P. Tarcher Inc. 1983)
Menon, T., *Backstage with Steven Wilson* (Rolling Stone India, June 2012)
Wilson, S., *Steven Wilson – Voyage 34 (The Future Bites Sessions)* (YouTube December 2020)

The Sky Moves Sideways
Clemons, P., *A chat with Steven Wilson late 1994* (Coventry Music Articles Blogspot republished 2017)
Gilmour, D., *My moon-landing jam session* (The Guardian, 2 July 2009)

Signify
Clarke, A., *No Hand was Visible: The Wall Writings at Borley Rectory* (The Foxearth and District Local History Society, 2003)

Office for National Statistics (UK), *Internet access – households and individuals, Great Britain* (August 2020)
Pautasso, L., *(Interview) STEVEN WILSON* (Reverb online, August 2016)
Ross, D., *s107: Sources of voice samples in music* (asciirose.com)
Unidentified author(s) *Music/Porcupine Tree/Drone of Dread* (TV Tropes website)
Women's History Network, *The History of Hemlines* (September 2003)

Stupid Dream
Ezell, B., *Prog's Only Stupid Dream: Porcupine Tree – "A Smart Kid"* (PopMatters, May 2012)
Kranitz, J., Henderson, K., *Porcupine Tree Review/Interview* (Aural innovations #7, July 1999)
Sander, E., *Porcupine Tree – Stupid Dream* (DPRP.net, December 1999)

Lightbulb Sun
Applewhite, M., *Last Chance to Evacuate Earth Before It's Recycled*; Edited Transcript of Videotape (Heaven's Gate website, September 29 1996)
Bredius, M., *Interview with Steven Wilson (Untitled)* (From Official Porcupine Tree website, originally published in Classic Rock Society Magazine, June 2000)
Dick, C., *Edited version of an interview with Steven Wilson* (From Official Porcupine Tree website, originally published in Eclipse Magazine, issues 5 and 6, USA, February 2001)
FaceCulture, *Steven Wilson interview (part 1)* (YouTube January 2015)
Jahlmar, J., *An Interview with Steven Wilson of Porcupine Tree* (DPRP.net, March 2001)
Kahn, S., *Colin Edwin: Porcupine Tree's bassist has a halo around his prog head* (MusicPlayers.com December 2010)
MacDonald, I., *Revolution in the Head: The Beatles and the Sixties* (Revised edition, Pimlico 1995)
Pardo, P., *Hailed for many years as the 'next big thing', can this influential and unique band break into the mainstream? An intimate chat with Steven Wilson* (Sea of Tranquility November 2001)
Press release, *HEAVEN'S GATE "Away Team" Returns to Level Above Human in Distant Space* (22 March 1997)
Space Rocks Live Forum, *Uplink 28: Music and Time Travel With Steven Wilson* (YouTube November 2020)

In Absentia
Everley, D., *In Ascendia* (Prog magazine, Issue 111, August 2020)
Prasad, A., *Porcupine Tree – Shadows and Light* (Innerviews.org 2004)
Reesman, B., *Porcupine Tree* (MixOnline.com April 2003)

Deadwing
Gray, A., *Steven Wilson interviewed* (SMNnews.com, March 2005, posted on the Porcupine Tree website)
Koolen, M., Van der Vorst, B.J., *Fear of a Dull Band* (DPRP.net 2008)
MarBelle, *Directors Notes Podcast 009 Deadwing – Mike Bennion* (November 2006)
Mettler, M., *Tracking Surround: Bristling at Stereo with Porcupine Tree's Steven Wilson* (soundandvision.com, September 2005)
Myspace Deadwing microsite (archived)

Prasad, A., *Porcupine Tree – Cinematic Catharsis* (Innerviews.org 2005)
Prasad, A., *Porcupine Tree Dream Logic* (Innerviews.org 2010)
Wilson S., Bennion, M., *And No Birds Sing (Teaser)* (Trailer for proposed new film version of *Deadwing*) (YouTube September 2020)

Fear of a Blank Planet

Cloutier, C., *Progressive Rock Gets Mordantly Witty* (NPR Song of the Day, 4 June 2007)
Ellis, Bret Easton, *Lunar Park* (Picador 2005)
Kelly, J., *Steven Wilson of Porcupine Tree* (ProgArchives.com April 2007)
Koolen, M., Van der Vorst, B. J., *Fear of a Dull Band* (*DPRP.net* 2008)
Kscope Podcast, *Gavin Harrison on 'Cheating the Polygraph'* (Episode 61 March 2015 presented by Billy Reeves)
Povarchik, R., *Interview with Porcupine Tree lead guitarist/singer/songwriter Steven Wilson* (alternative-zine.com June 2007)
Smith, S., *In the Court of King Crimson* (Panegyric revised edition 2019)
Wickel, C., *Porcupine Tree – Steven Wilson, 2007* (Guest Musicalypse, November 2007)
YouTube, *FaceCulture Interview with Steven Wilson (Porcupine Tree)* (August 2009)

Nil Recurring

Prasad, A., *Porcupine Tree Dream Logic* (Innerviews.org 2010)

The Incident

Conaton, C., *Porcupine Tree: The Incident* (PopMatters, October 2009)
Ebert, R., *Review of the movie Crash by David Cronenberg* (RogerEbert.com, 21 March 1997)
Pautasso, L., *An Inspirational 'Incident': An Interview with Musical Mastermind, Steven Wilson 27th August 2009* (lilen11.wordpress.com)
Prasad, A., *Porcupine Tree Dream Logic* (Innerviews.org 2010)
Prasad, A., *Porcupine Tree – Cinematic Catharsis* (Innerviews.org 2005)
Service, T., *Symphony guide: John Adams's Harmonielehre* (The Guardian, 11 March 2014)
YouTube, *FaceCulture Interview with Steven Wilson (Porcupine Tree)* (August 2009)
YouTube, *Roadrunner Records Porcupine Tree – The Incident Track by Track Parts I and II* (25 November 2009)

Recordings

CD sleeve notes
Fitzgerald, J., *Porcupine Tree – Recordings* (Aural Innovations #18, January 2002)

Also recommended

Wilson, R., *Time Flies: The Story of Porcupine Tree* (Rocket 88, 2017)
Tkach, G. M., Sieker, P. M., Madinger, C., *Steven Wilson Footprints Volume I Early Years and Porcupine Tree* (G & P Publishing 2021)